Bologna

Footprint

Ben Donald

4   About the author
4   Acknowledgements

5 Introducing Bologna
  6   Introduction
  8   At a glance
 12   Trip planner
 15   Contemporary Bologna

21 Travel essentials
 23   Getting there
 27   Getting around
 29   Tours and tourist information

Guide

31 Bologna
 33   Centre: piazza Maggiore and around
 48   Northeast: the University Quarter
 65   Southeast: Santo Stefano and around
 79   Southwest: around via del Pratello
 84   Northwest: around via Galliera
 90   Exhibition Centre and around
 93   Hills to the south

103 Around Bologna
 105   Apennine villages
 107   Parma
 110   Modena
 112   Ferrara
 115   Imola
 117   Ravenna
 117   Rimini

Listings

119 Sleeping
135 Eating and drinking
169 Bars and clubs
187 Arts and entertainment
    189 Cinema
    189 Comedy
    190 Music
    192 Theatre
193 Festivals and events
197 Shopping
205 Sports
211 Gay and lesbian
215 Kids
219 Directory

227 Background
    228 A sprint through history
    232 Art and architecture
    236 Books
    238 Language

242 Index
247 Publishing stuff

250 Maps
    250 Map 1
    252 Map 2
    254 Map 3
    256 Map 4

Around Bologna map (inside back cover)

About the author

Ben Donald is a freelance travel writer whose journalism has appeared in the (London) Times and various travel magazines such as Traveller, Global Adventure and Travel Africa. He is a keen independent traveller, fluent in a number of languages, including Italian and has lived and worked in a number of countries. During a year in Turin he really got under the skin of the Italian culture and all its beautiful and frustrating paradoxes.

Acknowledgements

I would like to thank: Ali at TalkaBOout for having her finger on the pulse and particularly in researching the bars and clubs section; my mate Chris at Hotel Spira for his unflagging and spontaneous hospitality and for his companionship in researching the best restaurants, bars and clubs for you; and lastly Merida, for putting up with the many absences during my research and all the lonely evenings while I transformed my notes into this book.

With streets like embroidered cloth, threaded with the arches of continuous colonnades, the heart of Bologna is a giant cloister. Under processions of classical columns and in the shadows cast between the half-moons of its winding alleys, the city inspires a furtive combination of intimacy and wandering, revealing her secrets to the unhurried visitor prepared to be led astray. Above and behind the chiaroscuro porticoes Bologna is a rose-red city of bombastic churches and vainglorious palaces, lasting testaments to the architectural flattery bestowed by the papal and civic forces that vied for control of the city. Striving for immortality, these patriarchs commissioned lavish chapels, frescoes and tombs, creating in the process one of the most influential schools of Italian art and bequeathing to the city a litter of monuments and masterpieces. These remain in good condition and accesssible, not ominously *sotto restauro*, as elsewhere in Italy.

The learned and the red

Although all roads might lead to Rome, they almost certainly pass through Bologna on the way. On a plain between the Apennine Mountains and the Adriatic Coast, Bologna has always been a strategic city. But it was also the city's propensity for free thinking that invaders wanted to control. Bologna has always been the Italian residence of pioneering thought, earning it the soubriquet, Bologna *la dotta* (the learned). Around the same time as Bolognese physicist Guglielmo Marconi, was discovering radio, Bologna became the birthplace and home of the Italian political Left. Already dubbed *la rossa* (the red) for its famed red buildings, Bologna's second nickname gained a more figurative meaning.

Raw ham and Ferraris

Today Bologna is the capital of Emilia-Romagna, a region of fertile plains, beautiful mountain scenery and a stretch of coastline that has long been a mecca for clubbers and sun-worshippers. It is also known for the cultural and material affluence of its other historic cities such as Modena, Parma, Ferrara and Ravenna and the many favourite Italian things they have become synonymous with: from the famous Parmesan cheese and Parma ham to the favourite industries of fast cars and fashion, Ferrari and Furla among those reinforcing the stereotypes of Italian boys and girls.

The fat of the land

The roar of engines, however, takes place mostly away from the ivory towers of the city – Bologna is a place for strolling and talking, if only to walk off one of the city's famous meals. The city is without doubt the stomach, if not the taste buds, of the country. The Bolognese have always taken the cultivation, preparation and consumption of their food very seriously, providing a very palatable edge to their socialism and earning the city its final affectionate appellation, Bologna *la grassa* (the fat).

At a glance

The heart of Bologna is still its Roman core, piazza Maggiore, at the confluence of the city's two main roads, via Ugo Bassi and via Rizzoli. These two roads are the contemporary face of the old Roman road, via Emilia, which once traversed the whole of the region. The area now referred to as the Centro Storico or old centre is defined by the *circonvallazione*: the busy main perimeter road which follows the line of the city's old extremity walls, joining up the 12 city gates.

Centre: piazza Maggiore and around

The pulse of the city and reference point for any visitor is its main square. Buffered at one end by the unfinished Gothic aspect of the Basilica di San Petronio and enclosed by the arcades and crenellations of squat edifices to Bologna's past prowess, this grandiose square is now a backdrop to a human theatre of poseurs and street artists. The perimeter of piazza Maggiore and the area beyond its eastern flanks called the Quadrilatero once constituted the entire extent of the original Roman settlement. The Quadrilatero is now a grid of teeming market streets full of colours, smells and bustle by day, and lively chic bars by night.

Northeast: the university quarter

Northeast of piazza Maggiore, down via Rizzoli and beyond the *due torri* (two towers) that have become the city's icon is the anarchic and bohemian atmosphere of via Zamboni and the heart of studentland. Along this street are the main faculty buildings and museums of Europe's oldest university and a dense concentration of bars and cafés under its porticoes. Returning west along via delle Belle Arti one finds La Pinacoteca, home to the largest collection of masterpieces by the Bolognese masters.

Tucked in just north of via Rizzoli are the sheer backalleys of Bologna's former Jewish Ghetto, still redolent of the suspicion that reigned in the 1500s. Further north around via Piella and via Cattani are some of Bologna's less-visited streets, offering a slice of local working-class life and, in a sliver of the old under-city waterway, a glimpse of the city's concealed past. Beyond them is piazza VIII Agosto and the Montagnola gardens, which come alive on Fridays and Saturdays, attracting crowds to the city's fleamarket. Returning south to piazza Maggiore along the main drag of via dell'Indipendenza is the city's cavernous cathedral.

Southeast: Santo Stefano and around

The three arteries of via Santo Stefano, via Castiglione and Strada Maggiore that lead southeast from piazza Maggiore make up the most tranquil and picturesque part of town. You can stroll up and down endless arcades enjoying the shifting perspectives of palatial buildings as they are framed by each arch. At their heart is the Santo Stefano complex of interconnecting churches, a maze of cloisters and chapels, each more intricate than the first.

Southwest: via d'Azeglio and via del Pratello

Leading due south from piazza Maggiore, the elegant via d'Azeglio and its capillaries are a catwalk where Bologna's glamourpusses and gatsbys prowl in search of the latest in chic from the city's alphabet of designer label stores. Further west, beyond the jagged edges of San Francesco church lies the seedy district of via del Pratello, Bologna's former red light district, whose concentration of late-night drinking dives and divers has earned it a popularity among those with a *nostalgie de la boue*.

Northwest: around via Galliera

Via dell'Indipendenza, Bologna's noisy main thoroughfare, bore the brunt of the Allied bombardments of the Second World War and despite subsequent reconstruction the area feels generally cold and angular though via Galliera has always been considered dark blue on the local Monopoly board. Hidden under via del Porto and at Porta Lame are the docks, where goods from as far north as the Po arrived via the nearby river Reno and the city's network of canals. These redundant industrial spaces are being reclaimed by the city's youth and transformed into clubs and cultural centres, making this area, at night, one of Bologna's most genuinely urban.

Exhibition Centre and around

North of the old city centre in a dedicated trade fair zone you can find a statement of Bologna's eye to the future: a modern urban landscape of glass and aluminium in contrast to the city's predominantly classical lines. Bologna has a calendar of fairs for industries as varied as underwear, modern art, cars and futurology. Nearby is the Ducati factory and museum.

Hills to the south

Bologna lies in the lee of the Apennines, whose verdant foothills creep up to the south of the city, concealing rustic villages and extravagant villas in their undulations. Atop one such hill stands Bologna's guardian, the sanctuary of the Madonna di San Luca, connected to the city by a colonnade of 666 arches. Energetic pilgrims are rewarded with magnificent views of the red city below.

Excursions

Emilia-Romagna holds many treasures, from historic and cultural centres such as Ferrara, seat of the famous Este dynasty and the Byzantine ruins of Ravenna to gastronomic wonders in the cheese-making factories of Parma and national parks in the Apennines where you can trek, wildlife-watch or ski. Automotive past and present can be seen at the famous Ferrari testing track and museum at Maranello near Modena or at the grand prix circuit at Imola. Or if you just want to chill out, why not head east and dip your toes in the Adriatic or take part in the national sport of phototropism at one of the beaches around Rimini?

Ten of the best

Best

1 **Basilica di San Petronio** Unfinished façade and vast interior containing many chapels and an outsize sundial, p34.

2 **Chiesa di Santo Stefano** Complex of seven interwoven churches, adorned with fine art and enclosed within cloisters. One of the most tranquil spots in the city, p69.

3 **Le Due Torri** From the top of the Torre Asinelli, one of Bologna's iconic twin towers, enjoy breathtaking views over the city's rooftops and the surrounding countryside, p49.

4 **La Pinacoteca Nazionale** Superb collection of paintings by Bolognese masters and others, including Giotto, p60.

5 **Portico and Santuario di San Luca** Bologna's shrine on the hill is accessed by a continuous colonnade of 666 arches. The panoramic views are spectacular, p93.

6 **San Giacomo Maggiore and l'Oratorio di Santa Cecilia** One of Bologna's most elegant and significant churches, with the hidden treasure of a cycle of scenes by Costa, Francia and Aspertini, p53.

7 **Chiesa di San Domenico** A beautiful church famous for the *arca*, the ornate canopy for the tomb of Saint Dominic and for its many lavish chapels, p57.

8 **Chiesa di Santa Maria dei Servi** An unmissable church for the wonderfully delicate quadrangle of neo-classical arcades that surround its small square, p71.

9 **Il Quadrilatero and Il Mercato di Mezzo** This ancient Roman grid of streets is a feast for the eyes and noses of those who have come to Bologna for its fabled food, p42.

10 **Oratorio della Chiesa della Madonna Colombano** Private chamber where the masters of the Bolognese school experimented with colour and form to startling effect, p87.

Trip planner

Italy's climate makes it an attractive holiday or short-break proposition virtually all year round. Bologna can get extremely hot between May and September. There can also be regular and spectacular downpours of rain, especially in spring and autumn. In both cases the city's arcades really come into their own for shelter and shade. If there is a bad time to visit, it is August when many of the city's museums, buildings and – worse still – restaurants close, sometimes for the whole month, sometimes just for the middle two weeks. All year round, visitors staying for a long weekend are advised to make the most of the weekend days as many sights, shops and restaurants close on a Monday.

A weekend (2-4 days)

Most of Bologna's main attractions are within a short walk of each other. However, there might be a temptation to cram in too many sights. Time is equally enjoyably spent simply strolling around the arcaded streets. That said, a weekend visit will comfortably allow for a snapshot of the principal sights in the heart of Bologna's old centre while still allowing time for shopping and lounging in cafés. Starting in piazza Maggiore, these might include: a look inside the Basilica di San Petronio and a climb up the Torre Asinelli before a wander around the streets of the university quarter down via Zamboni and into the beautiful church and oratory of San Giacomo Maggiore before ending up in the Pinacoteca gallery, the best introduction to the Bolognese school of art. If it is Friday or Saturday, the market on piazza VIII Agosto will make a lively antidote to the art. You should also make time for a look around the serene cloisters of the Santo Stefano church complex. Finally you'll probably want to walk off all the mortadella by taking a Sunday stroll up the colonnade to the shrine of San Luca where you can enjoy panoramic views over the city and lower Apennines.

One week or more

A week will give you time to enjoy the above essential sights at a more leisurely pace and linger in some of the city's interesting districts such as the Mirasoli at the end of via Castiglione, the via del Pratello and the canal area around via delle Moline. You might also want to inspect the treasures of the chiesa di San Domenico and the magical hidden Chiesa della Madonna del Colombano in via Parigi. If you go up to the shrine at San Luca, the surrounding hills offer many lovely parks, monasteries and villas such as Parco di Villa Ghigi and San Michele in Bosco.

Bologna is also an excellent springboard for day trips or even one-night stop-overs to Italian cities such as Modena and Ferrara. Parma and its world-famous cheese and ham is less than an hour away, as is the coastal resort of Rimini. Ferraris are made just up the road at Maranello and raced on the grand-prix circuit at Imola just south of Bologna, while the hills southwest of Bologna offer spa towns, trekking and winter skiing, all within easy reach by both public and private transport.

Such is the embarrassment of choice you may wish to organize your visit into themes, such as art, food, technology, or just shopping.

Churches, art and architecture

Be daunted by the basilica of San Petronio, awestruck by the delicate interwoven churches of Santo Stefano (p69). See the abundance of sculptures and fresoces by Bolognese and Renaissance masters in San Martino (p61), San Domenico (p57), San Giacomo Maggiore (p53) and Giovanni in Monte (p72). Discover the exquisite secrets upstairs in the Chiesa della Madonna del Colombano (p87). Get an overload of Bolognese masters at the city art gallery, La Pinacoteca (p60) and the Collezioni Comunali d'Arte in the Palazzo Comunale (p38). For a trip into modernity, visit the Galleria d'Arte Moderna (p89) and the Museo Morandi (p39) dedicated to Bologna's answer to Cezanne.

Museum passes

A yearly pass (*abbonamento*), good value if you are staying for more than a weekend or plan to return, is €25 and allows unlimited access to Bologna's museums. Visitors staying for a shorter period might find the *biglietto cumulativo* (one or three day passes) better, costing €6 and €8 respectively. For €14 you can also buy a *biglietto integrato*, valid for three days and allowing you access to the museums and also use of public transport. **T** 051-203040 for further information.

Food
Take a culinary tour of the city's delicatessens, central and outlying restaurants. See fresh pasta being made outside Trattoria Anna Maria (p144). Visit the food markets of the Quadrilatero, especially Tamburini (p201). Visit the cheese factories of Parma (p106).

Technology
Visit the Ducati museum, the Ferrari museum at Maranello and the Formula One circuit at Imola (p116). Go to the university museums and relive the pioneering of Marconi and Galvani (p56). Visit the Exhibition Centre of the Quartiere Fieristico and attend one of Bologna's many important trade fairs, especially the Motor Show and Futureshow (p91).

Shopping
Shop and window-shop in an array of classy, chic and costly designer stores around town (p200). Seek out some more hip and experimental stores offering innovative Italian takes on London grunge (p200).

Contemporary Bologna

Innovation, liberal thought and rebellion – three characteristics linked by a common challenge to the status quo, have always characterized the spirit of Bologna and its citizens. Bologna was always a restless subject of Popes, kings and ruling dynasties and its medieval history is littered with uprisings, overthrowings and general disobedience to attempted foreign authorities. The city's university, the first of its kind in Europe, was always an engine of enlightenment and discovery, from the first principles of European Law and human rights to the invention of radio. And the Bolognese rejection of Mannerism, born of an innate pragmatism, founded one of the most influential schools of classical art. These three characteristics still manifest themselves today, in a different guise, running under the surface of modern life in Bologna and connecting the city to its past.

   Bologna's position at the forefront of Italian technology continues to this day. Twinned with Coventry in the UK, it seems apposite that Bologna and its environs are sometimes referred to as *la terra delle moto* – the land of motorbikes – due to the concentration of car and motorbike factories located around the city. That's about as far as the comparison can stretch, though. Apart from the significant difference in architectural beauty between Bologna and its Midlands relative, the factories in question are none other than Ducati, Ferrari, Lamborghini and Maserati. Personally I'd rather be sent to Bologna.

   Independent, specialist and small or medium-sized companies, these famous stables are also typical of the type of business to be found in Bologna, and different from the cumbersome conglomerates further north. These industries have contributed to make Bologna and its surrounds one of the most affluent regions in the country – dubbed the 'Third Italy' between the industrial triangle in the north and the underdeveloped South.

   Bologna is also known for its innovation in the field of fashion, and in particular *pronta moda* or off-the-peg fashion. A quick glance in the clothes shops along via dell'Indipendenza will also reveal an experimental-grunge for young and trendy Bolognese more akin to London, and a far cry from the rigidity of Barbours, V-neck jumpers and brown brogues seemingly *de rigueur* elsewhere in Italy. It is said that many of the designs that end up on the catwalks of Milan started out as experimental ideas in Bologna. Remember, you saw it first here.

Bolognese innovation in youth fashion has also translated into the city's bars, cafés and nightclubs. When it comes to concept bars and wacky décors Bologna has a greater selection than many Italian cities, reclaiming its former industrial zones and warehouses, especially to the northwest, with some surprising results. Also contrary to the profoundly conservative currents running through the country, Bologna has a renowned and well-organized gay scene – a further statement of its emancipated attitude. The funky bars and clubs are packed with Bologna's arty-camp population, mixing easily with more red-blooded revellers.

Many bars serve also as stages for the city's abundant artists, combining eating and drinking with short film projections, exhibitions, performance art, music, theatre and dance spectacles. Bologna and Emilia-Romagna also have a long tradition of music. Nearby Parma hosts opera productions to rank alongside those of La Scala or Verona, and Modena is birthplace of Luciano Pavarotti. Nowadays the city is, by Italian standards, a centre for jazz, hosting many international line-ups in its clubs and providing a forum for newcomers. Rock music is alive and kicking in Bologna, too. Birthplace of Lucio Dalla and Italy's only real rocker, Vasco Rossi, the city is a stop on the tours of many international pop acts. In 2000 Bologna was nominated a European City of Culture and like a latter-day patriarch, the progressive city council is very active in its support of artistic initiatives. The lengths of via Zamboni, the self-professed street of art and via delle Belle Arti are plastered with posters announcing the latest events going on in the city, from raves to recitals of poetry.

Many of these local artists and performers are students, following in the lofty footsteps of such alumni as Dante, Boccaccio and Petrarch, but also of the enraged and engaged students who took Bologna's university into the political sphere. After the end of the Second World War, and as if in rebellion against the memory of its recent fascist occupation, Bologna became the centre of Socialism in Italy. From that moment on, and particularly during Italy's dark years of terrorism in the 1970s and 1980s, the city was a mouthpiece for a voice uncomfortable to a centre-right government accused by many, such as the journalist and film director Pier Paolo Pasolini, of creeping fascism. In 1977 Bologna's 70,000-strong student population took to the streets in a revolt that was their own local version of 1968. In 1980 the city became a target and received a vendetta from neo-fascist far right terrorists in the form of a massive bomb attack on the station, which killed 80 people.

Things have changed a bit since those days of meaningful activism and anarchy. Nowadays the long hair is still there, the graffiti and the bicycles, but Bologna's seemingly eternally resting modern-day students could be accused of living the image of the artist-rebel without the belief and direction of their predecessors. Nor is the city these days considered such a bastion of protest and left-wing principles of philanthropy, austerity and abstention. Then perhaps this was always the city's alluring and ultimately workable paradox. Bologna is a land of plenty, totally devoted to epicurean pleasures, whose affluence, gluttony and famed corpulence, to say nothing of its fast cars and fashion, rather take the edge off its social conscience and belie the image of the starving student. If there are any *partigiani* (partisans) left, they are more than likely of the *prosecco* variety.

Which brings us to the city's most famous ingredient – its food. Despite other regions' claims, Bologna's cuisine is the best in Italy. Cultivated, prepared, served and consumed with great pride and sensual pleasure but minimum ritual, food and wine have been Bologna's real religion since the city's foundation. Over this time

Cholesterol capital
Bologna's food shops are exhibits of the city's culinary arts.

the Bolognese have invented a tongue-twisting delicatessen and oral orgy of pastas, meats, cheese and sauces, from tagliatelle and tortellini to mortadella and squacquerone, to name just a few. And as they have invented them, so these dishes have passed into the region's tradition. But while today's chefs respect and vaunt their city's culinary heritage they also perceive their vocation as a process of development, a moveable or at least evolving feast, ripe for innovation. We're not talking fusion of Japanese with Moroccan food here, but specialities of the house, with subtle and significant nuances on traditional themes. The famed spirit of innovation and experimentation is expanding the territory of the city's gastronomic traditions, discovering new Dionysian delights to satisfy both gourmet and glutton.

Travel essentials

Bologna is easily and economically accessible from the UK: the cheapest flights to the city are from London Stansted either with Go direct to Bologna airport, or with Ryanair who fly to Forlì, 45 km to the southeast.

There is no underground, but a very efficient bus system, though generally, your feet is all you'll need. The most Bolognese method for getting around the city (and by far the most fun) is either by bicycle or moped. Both these will allow access to Bologna's back streets and hidden sights. A good-value and reasonably efficient network of public transport can take you on trips out into the hills or to the surrounding cities of Parma, Ferrara, Imola, Modena and to the sea at Rimini.

If you'd like somebody to show you around, informative walking tours take you to the some of the less-discovered corners of the city, bus tours give your legs a rest, and wine and food tasting tours are a good excuse for more copious consumption of the area's produce. You can even orientate yourself by going up in a balloon.

Getting there

Air

From UK and Europe Both *Go* and *Ryanair* have fares starting at around £80 return if you book early enough, to Bologna and Forlì airports respectively. A small discount is offered for bookings made online. There are frequent scheduled flights on *British Airways* and *Alitalia* to Bologna from London's Heathrow and Gatwick airports, usually costing upwards of £150 return (although *British Airways* has introduced newer, competitive fares starting at £99 return). Bologna is also connected by direct flights to many European cities including Amsterdam, Barcelona, Brussels, Copenhagen, Frankfurt, Lyon, Lisbon, Madrid, Nice, Paris, Prague, Vienna and Zurich.

From North America There are no direct flights to Bologna from the US or Canada. It is, however, relatively cheap to fly via London or another European hub, such as Frankfurt or Zurich. Other options are the routings via Milan or Rome. The cheaper end of the scale costs from $500-600 upwards off-season, rising to over $1000 in the popular summer months.

→ **Airlines and agents**

Alitalia, **T** 0874-5448259, www.alitalia.it
British Airways, **T** 0845-7733377, www.ba.com
Go , **T** 0870-6076543, www.go-fly.com
Ryanair, **T** 0870-1569569, www.ryanair.com
Virgin Atlantic, **T** 01293-450150, www.fly.virgin.com
Expedia, **T** 0870-0500808, www.expedia.com
LastMinute, www.lastminute.com
STA Travel, **T** 0870-1600599, www.sta-travel.com
Travelocity, **T** 0870-8763876, www.travelocity.com
Trailfinders, **T** 020-79371234, www.trailfinders.com

From Australia and New Zealand There are no direct flights to Bologna (or anywhere else in Italy) from either Australia or New Zealand. You will have to change at least twice. You can fly to Milan and Rome via another European or Asian (eg Singapore, Kuala Lumpur) city, from where you will have to connnect again for Bologna. Airlines that fly to European cities from Australia and New Zealand include: *Alitalia, British Airways, Lufthansa, Malaysian Airlines, Qantas, Singapore Airlines* and *Virgin Atlantic*. The cost low season is likely to be at least A$1,700, rising to A$2,500 during high season.

Getting to and from the airports Bologna's **Marconi International Airport** (**T** 051-6479615 (0630-2330), **F** 051-6479719, www. bologna-airport.it) is 6 km northwest of the city centre. There are two passenger terminals. All arrivals come in to terminal A. European and domestic departures leave from Terminal A while intercontinental departures leave from terminal B. Recently upgraded, the airport has facilities for changing money, a bank, restaurant, newsagent, snack bars and various shops selling gifts, books and souvenirs. There is a large and helpful tourist information desk in the centre of the arrivals hall, stacked with leaflets and serviced by English-speaking staff. All the major car hire companies also have offices here. Business facilities have recently been installed.

The best way to the centre is by taxi from the rank outside the terminal A. A taxi to the centre normally costs around €12-15, depending on traffic. Alternatively, the Bologna Aerobus (**T** 051-290290) also connects the airport to the city centre. It runs every 15 minutes from 0520 to midnight and takes about 20 minutes. Tickets cost €4.50 and are sold on board.

Forlì is a small and rudimentary airport that has not yet caught up with its status as a budget airline destination and gateway to Bologna, or with the associated increase in international traffic (**T** 0543-474990, **F** 0543-474909, www.forli-airport.it). There is a direct bus service from Forlì airport to Bologna's bus station (on piazza XX Settembre next to the train station) which is timetabled to coincide with incoming flights from London, leaving 30 minutes after each flight's arrival and waiting in case of delay. It takes around 1 hour 15 minutes and costs €10 per person – buy tickets on board. There is no direct train connection between Forlì airport and Bologna so you have to go into Forlì itself. A municipal bus (€0.80) departs from the airport every 20 minutes and takes around 15 minutes to reach the train station from where connections to Bologna can be found. Provincial trains leave for Bologna every half hour or so, take about 40 minutes and cost around €3 each way. For the return, the direct buses from Bologna to Forlì airport depart once a day at 1230, Mon-Fri, 1520 on Sat and 1315 on Sun, again to coincide with necessary check-in times for departing international flights.

Road

Car Italy has an excellent network of *autostrade* (motorways) that in a country which is two-thirds mountain often involve amazing feats of engineering. Bologna is linked by the A1 to Milan (2 hours), Florence (1 hour) and Rome (three hours), by the A13 to Venice and Padua and the A14 to Rimini, Ravenna and the Adriatic coast. All motorways are tolled (eg driving from Rome to Bologna costs approximately €15, travellers on a budget might therefore prefer the *strade statali* or *SS*) which are toll-free dual carriageways. The nominal speed limit is 130 km for motorways and 110 km/h on SS, although both are conspicuously flouted by the natives. EU nationals taking their own vehicle need an International Insurance Certificate, also known as a *carta verde* (green card). For more information on this contact *Automobile Club Italiano* (**T** 06-49981, 24hrs). Emergency breakdown (ACI) **T** 116.

Bus/coach It's an arthritis-guaranteeing ride but for the truly budget conscious Bologna can be reached by coach from London Victoria station in about 24 hours (£71 return, contact *Eurolines UK Ltd*, **T** 08705-143219, www.gobycoach.com). Within Italy services connect the city to both Milan and Ancona in the south. Regional coaches, ambitiously called *pullman service* go to Ferrara and Modena. All coaches depart and arrive from the coach station in piazza XX Settembre (**T** 051-247134) just round the corner from the train station.

Train

Bologna station (Bologna Centrale) is at piazza Medaglie d'Oro (**T** 051-630211) to the north of the city. Several car hire companies (Avis, Hertz, Maggiore) have offices here and other facilities include banks, bars, restaurants, newspaper stalls and a pharmacy. The heart of the city is a 15 minute walk up via dell'Indipendenza. Alternatively take bus 10, 25 or 30 (purchase a ticket from *tabacchi* (tobacconists) designated by a white 'T' in a black box outside the shops. For timetable information and bookings contact TrenItalia on **T** 199-166177 (from within Italy) or visit www.trenitalia.com

Bologna is a major junction on Italy's railway network, making it very accessible to other Italian cities and European destinations further afield. Italy's own Eurostar currently links Bologna to Milan (2 hours), Florence (1 hour), Rome (3 hours) and Naples (5 hours) while the Eurocity connects passengers with more than 40 other European destinations including Paris, Basel and Brussels. The Italian state railway, recently rebranded *TrenItalia*, is more efficient than mythology would have it. It is also one of the most economical in Europe, fares in both directions being charged by the kilometre. Once bought, a ticket is not valid until stamped before boarding in one of the yellow machines on the platform. There are five types of train, divided according to speed and the frequency with which they stop. Diretto, Inter-regionale and Espresso all stop frequently and only require a standard ticket whereas supplements are usually required on the faster Intercity and Eurostar services.

Getting around

Central Bologna is easily covered on foot. It takes just under an hour to walk from one side of the Centro Storico to the other.

Bicycle and moped
Bologna's bikes are the honest, old-fashioned, sit-up-and-beg type, robust enough to withstand the cobbles. Expect to be looked at quizzically if you ask for a helmet, such things not yet having been absorbed into the Italian image. Impassable, narrow streets make Bolognese cyclists relatively immune to fast traffic, however, so you should be ok. Bikes and mopeds can be hired from *Abycar*, piazza Medaglie d'Oro 3, **T** 051-253832 or *Senzauto*, also at the train station, **T** 051-251401. Prices start at €5.20 per day for a bicycle (*bicicletta*) and €32 per day for a scooter (*motorino*). A deposit of €150 or €515 respectively is payable.

Bus
The centre and suburbs are covered by an efficient network of orange buses run by the *ATC* (*Trasporti Pubblici Bologna*, **T** 051-290290, www.atc.bo.it). Information on services can be found in the train and coach station in piazza XX Settembre as well as at their city office on via Marconi. A simple ticket costs €1 and lasts an hour from the time you validate it in the machine upon boarding. Within this time you can use the same ticket on as many buses and for as many journeys as you wish. Alternatively, and better value, the City Pass is valid for up to seven journeys (of up to one hour each) across multiple days and costs €5. There is also a *giornaliero* (day ticket) which costs €3 and lasts 24 hours from validation. All bus tickets can be purchased at *tabacchi* (tobacconists/newsagents – marked with a 'T' outside), bars and newspaper kiosks. For information on services see the above website or call **T** 051-290290, 0700-2000.

   Controllori intermittently patrol the buses in blue uniforms or sometimes plain clothes. The penalty for not having a valid ticket is around €50, payable on the spot.

Buses leave the coach station in piazza XX Settembre every hour for Ferrara and take 45 minutes. They leave every 15 minutes for Imola and take an hour. There are also regular buses to Parma. Tickets to all these cost in the region of €12-20 return.

Car

Unless you have arrived by car, driving in the city is to be avoided. The centre is compact and easily coverable on foot or with public transport. Parking is also very difficult. The Centro Storico is officially closed to private vehicles every day from 0700-2000 although this restriction does not apply to guests staying in the centre provided that they register with the police on arrival. Your hotel should be able to do this for you. Many hotels also have private parking for guests for which a supplement is usually charged. The city does operate a park and ride scheme, details of which are available from the *ATC* office (see p27).

Taxi

Taxis in Italy are generally expensive as drivers will find any excuse to justify various add-ons. If booked by phone you will be charged for the journey to pick you up. Although technically possible, do not try to hail a taxi in the street. You might as well be waving to someone on the other side. It's best to queue up at the ranks in piazza Maggiore or outside the train station, or better still, think ahead and book by phone via the city's taxi co-operative on **T** 051-372727.

Train

Trains run frequently from Bologna to Ferrara, Modena and Imola, all taking around half an hour. Ravenna is about 40 minutes by direct train, as is Rimini. Parma is about 45 minutes. There are also frequent trains from Ravenna to the coast. Tickets to all these destinations cost in the region of €8-12 single.

Tours and tourist information

Tours

Bus tours   A tour of Bologna in a 16-seater minibus is offered by
the company *Cosepuri*. The bus departs on Saturday and Sunday
only, leaving twice daily, at 1000 and 1500 from via dell'
Indipendenza (in front of the Scalinata Pincio), stopping to pick
up outside the Hotel Baglioni and in piazza Re Enzo. It takes two
hours, covering all the main sights with the help of a multilingual
guide and costs €10. Accompanied children under six go free. For
more information call **T** 051-517070. To book, call the same number the day before you want to do the tour. The same company
also offers bus tours of the surrounding towns and countryside.

Walking tours   Well-paced, informative multi-lingual walking
tours of the city are on offer. *Discover Bologna/Scopri Bologna*,
T 051-246541, departs at 1030 on Wednesdays, Saturday and

★ **Bologna by bike**
*Narrow streets and an (almost) traffic-free centre make bikes the ideal
and most Bolognese way to get around. They also double as a symbol
of the city's socialist aspirations.*

Sundays from the IAT (Ufficio Informazioni e Accoglienza Turistica), piazza Maggiore 1. *Prima Classe* (**T** 0347-8944094), departs at 1100 from the Fontana Nettuno on Sundays. Both cost €13 per person. GAIA (**T** 051-2960005) also organize guided tours. One-on-one guides arranged through *Associazione Guida d'Arte*, **T** 051-4210809 cost around €60 for three hours.

Bologna by balloon The *Aerostato-Osservatorio* (**T** 051-6448856, www.aerophile.it) is a static balloon which rises 150 m above the city from the Giardini Margherita (entrance off via Castiglione) offering great views over the towers and other monuments. Rides last 15 minutes and cost €11 , concessions €7 and accompanied children up to 12 years, €5.

Wine tours *Strada dei Vini e dei Sapori* (**T** 0542-25413, www.stradavinniesapori.it) offer food and wine-tasting tours into the villages and vineyards in the Apennine hills around Imola.

Tourist information
Other than the offices at the airport and train station, Bologna's main tourist office is under the Palazzo Podesta at piazza Maggiore 1, **T** 051-246541, www.comune.bologna.it/bolognaturismo *open every day from 0900-2000.*

It also contains the *Emporio della Cultura*, a tourist bookshop offering more maps and leaflets than you could possibly need and very friendly, multilingual service.

Ferrara Castello Estense, **T** 0532-209370. **Ravenna** via Salara 8/12, **T** 0544 482670, turismorav@provincia.ra.it **Modena** piazza Grande 17, **T** 059-206660, iatmo@comune.modena.it *Mon-Fri 0930-1230, 1530-1830. Sat 0930-1230.* **Parma** via Melloni 1B **T** 0521-218889, turismo@comune.parma.it, www.turismo.commune.parma.it **Rimini** piazzale F Fellini 3, **T** 0541-56902, iat2@iper.net *0900-1200, 1500-1900.*

Centre: piazza Maggiore and around 33

The two conjoining squares of piazza Maggiore and piazza Nettuno are the social hub of the city.

Northeast: the university quarter 48

A lively and bohemian atmosphere comprising 17th- and 18th-century palazzos, porticoed streets and intriguing alleys.

Southeast: Santo Stefano and around 65

Bologna's most picturesque, stately and tranquil district with a fascinating piazza at its heart.

Southwest: around via del Pratello 79

From the elegant catwalk of via d'Azeglio, to boozy uproarious *osterie*.

Northwest: around via Galliera 84

Modern concrete dotted with occasional old streets and a watery industrial underground history.

Exhibition centre and around 90

Shiny towers, trade fairs and modern art.

Hills to the south 93

The foothills of the Apennines begin just outside the city walls with villas, parks and the 666 arches of the Portico di San Luca.

Centre: piazza Maggiore and around

The space of piazza Maggiore exerts an almost magnetic pull on visitors and locals alike so that you will inevitably start or end up here. Standing in the middle of the entirely pedestrianized piazza you feel you could be in the central courtyard of a great castle, enclosed and protected by towers: the tall, thick and crenellated masses of the **Palazzo Comunale** *and* **Palazzo Podesta** *and the forbidding weight of the* **Basilica di San Petronio** *whose faceless façade makes it more resemble a fortification than a place of worship. The site of the ancient Roman forum, the city's most emblematic buildings are here. Until the 19th century the square was the city's main market place and it still teems with life, from wandering locals on their* passeggiata *to ant-like swarms of visiting school children. A perfect meeting place, the piazza also offers a wonderful shop window onto Italian life. Sit back and observe the Italians as they do what they do best: hanging around for no discernible reason but looking so cool and well-groomed for it not to matter. Apart from this daily social theatre, the piazza serves as Bologna's answer to Covent Garden and there is usually some freelance art show. A forum for coronations and executions in Roman times, the piazza now stages anything from puppet shows to the ubiquitous international Peruvian panpipe band.*

▸▸ *See Sleeping p121, Eating and drinking p138, Bars and clubs p171*

◉ Sights

Fontana del Nettuno
Map 4, D3, p256

Bologna's bronze statue of the Roman God of the Sea might as well have been conceived as a statue to the God of Photography, so much has it become a symbol of the city and a favourite backdrop for posing visitors who adorn the *putti* (chubby cherubs) and mermaids at his feet. Completed between 1563 and 1566 and known affectionately as *il Gigante* due to its size, the statue is the work of the Flemish sculptor known as Jean de Boulogne, or in Italian, Giambologna for the amount of time he spent working in the city, and is based on a design by Tommaso Laureti. The statue was commissioned by bishop Pier Donato Cesi as part of an urban beautification programme requested by the then Pope Pio IV and aimed at making Papal Bologna the second city in Italy after Rome. On the side of the Palazzo Comunale is another fountain, referred to as *la fontana vecchia* (old fountain), older than the Neptune fountain but also designed by Tommaso Laureti.

● *Legend has it that prior to commencing work on the design of the Fontana del Nettuno, and preoccupied with the ample nudity of the pagan God, Giambologna sought an approval from the Pope. "For Bologna it's ok" came the answer, an early confirmation of the city's fame in Italy as a centre for more liberal attitudes and emancipated thinking.*

★ Basilica di San Petronio
piazza Maggiore, **T** 051-225442. *0715-1300, 1430-1830 in winter, afternoon closing in summer. Free. Map 4, E3, p256*

The construction of Bologna's basilica to her patron saint was a project the expense of which it is hard to imagine would be tolerated by democracies nowadays. San Petronio cost both vast amounts of money and lives to build as well as the demolition of many churches and houses to make way for it. As the façade and half-arches down the western exterior tell, the ambition was never fully realized. Funded by public money, the basilica, which is a civic temple not a cathedral, was conceived by the elected city council as a monument of opposition to the Papacy in Rome and originally intended to be larger than St Peter's. The Papacy grew fearful of this ambition and diverted money and land elsewhere – to the construction of the Archiginnasio and founding of the university.

The models in the church **museum** in the annex (*T 051-223256, 1000-1200 except Tue and Thu, free*) show that what is currently standing is only one-fifth of a project that foresaw a longer nave, transept and a 150-m high dome. That said, at 132 m in length, it is still one of the largest churches in Christendom. Designed in a late Gothic style by the architect Antonio di Vicenzo, the first stone was laid in 1390 and the current state reached only after several centuries of labour. Aside from the lower arches down its side which were constructed from the stone of demolished houses, the pale, main bulk of the church is rather plain and unspectacular, emphasizing the deceit that would have been the façade had it been completed. Its base is embellished with stripes of red Veronese marble and white Istrian stone whereas the charcoal-coloured top two-thirds of the façade remain bare, giving the basilica a blunt aspect as ugly as it is intriguing.

The vast interior too seems empty and dour, with bodiless amplified supplications echoing around like platform announce-ments. That said, God is in the details and on closer inspection the basilica does have many redeeming features. The first of these are the unfinished figures in the half-moon above the central portal begun in 1425 by the Renaissance master Jacopo della Quercia depicting the Madonna and Child, Saint Petronius and Saint Ambrosius and, either side of the door, stories from the Old Testament. Just above the door there used also to be a rare bronze figurine of Pope Julius II made by Michelangelo in 1508. In an act of Ghibelline anti-Papal disrespect the figurine was plundered and melted down into ammunition for the wars between the Bentivoglio and Este dynasties. Meanwhile, also by de Quercia are the bas-reliefs on the nave pillars depicting stories from both the Old and New Testaments.

The basilica contains 22 side chapels with paintings, sculptures, glasswork, faience and marquetry by many Bolognese hands. Perhaps the most exquisite of these is the Capella Bolognini, financed by the Bolognini family's silk empire, with its frescoes by

Giovanni de Modena depicting the *Journey of the Three Kings*, *Paradise* and, most spectacularly, *Hell*.

The intact skull of Saint Petronius has been preserved above the altar while the astronomical clock created in 1655 by Gian Domenico Cassini and Domenico Guglielmi illustrates the links between the basilica and the city as a centre of exploration and discovery. As a direct result of their studies of Galileo's theories at the city's university the two men conceived of this outsize sundial whose length, precisely 67.72 m, equals 1/600,000th of the earth's circumference. At noon the sunlight entering by means of a hole in the ceiling hits this line and throughout the year travels from one end to the other, enabling measurement of the exact date of the summer and winter solstices. The marble slabs along the line indicate the days and months and also the signs of the zodiac. It was this line which led to the discovery of the anomalies in the Julian calendar (in 1532 the spring equinox arrived too early) and ultimately to the invention of leap years and the reform of the calendar by Pope Gregory XII, after whom the modern Gregorian calendar is named.

● *If you want refreshment and a rest for your neck after visiting the Basilica, avoid the crowds in the cafés on piazza Maggiore, duck into via Clavature and enjoy a cappuccino at Rosa Rose (see p172).*

Palazzo Comunale
piazza Maggiore 6, **T** 051-203526. *Tue-Sat 0930-1830, Sun 1000-1830, closed Mon. Entry to galleries €4.13. Map 4, C2-D3, p256*

As imposing as the basilica, it is hard to believe that the fortress-like citadel that occupies the entire west flank of piazza Maggiore, encompassing 15,000 sq m, is merely the city's town hall. Built in 1287, it is more like a small city within a city. Commissioned by Cardinal Anglic de Grimoard in 1336 to encircle the complex, the considerable defences were conceived as a show of strength by the Papacy and to defend it from warring Ghibellines. The building

★ Partisan memorial

During World War Two, Bologna's Nazi occupiers conducted a series of ruthless massacres of Bologna's resistance partisans, the most gruesome of which took place at Marzabotto to the west of the city. On the wall of the Palazzo Comunale are photographs of the victims.

is sometimes referred to as the Palazzo d'Accursio after the original owner of the real estate.

Other than for its sheer grandiosity, the building is notable for a number of outstanding features. The clocktower, and Bologna's answer to Big Ben, was built in 1773 by Rinaldo Gandolfi. The famous terracotta *Madonna and Child* which adorns the façade was completed in 1478 by a sculptor from Puglia, Nicola dell'Arca. The large classical groundfloor window is the design of Galeazzo Alessi (no relation to the juicer designer) below which are two marble eagles, the left of which is attributed to Michelangelo. On the wall below is a plaque which sets out the decreed standards of

★ Best places for coffee

Best

• Caffe Morandi, p153.
• Caffe de' Commercianti, p153
• Caffe del Teatro, p146
• Caffe la Torinese, p140

measurement in medieval times (the foot, the double arm and the perch) to avoid cheating and arguments between traders. Perhaps the most striking feature is the huge finger-wagging stature of Pope Gregory XIII produced by Menganti between 1576 and 1580. In contrast to many of Bologna's other main buildings, which are robust in their symbolic defiance of papal control, this statue, commissioned at a time when Bologna was controlled from Rome, was by its size designed to leave the citizens in no doubt as to who was boss. Ironically by the time of the Napoleonic invasions the Bolognese had become so proud of this symbol of their city, they dressed it up as Saint Petronius to save it from destruction by the French Emperor's anti-papal army.

The ground floor of the Palazzo was once used as a market and warehouse for grain. The magnificent tall first floor hall is reached via a beautiful passage with a sloping wooden causeway, so designed by Bramante for easy access by noblemen on horseback or in sedan chairs. At the top of these stairs is the Sala di Ercole ('Hercules' room', after the terracotta statue of the hero there by Lombardi). This room is decorated in beautiful frescoes, among which Tibaldi's *Vigiliance*, Ludovico Carracci's *Phaeton's Fall*, the *Madonna* by Lippo di Dalmasio and the *Madonna and the Earthquake* by Francesco Francia are the most famous. The inside courtyard contains interesting rooms, many of which are open to visitors. The most important of these is probably the **Sala Farnese**, home of the **Collezioni Comunali d'Arte**, the city public art collection which includes paintings and frescoes by many masters of the Bolognese school such as Signorelli, the Caracci brothers and di Paolo, and works by Tintoretto. Nowadays rooms of the Palazzo Comunale are used for a variety of events from receptions and functions to product launches, musical performances, temporary art exhibitions and even mild raves.

Museo Morandi

Palazzo Communale, piazza Maggiore 6, **T** 051-203646/203332. *1000-1800, Tue-Sun. Closed Mon. Entry €4.13.   Map 4, D2, p256*

Adjacent to the Sala Farnese within the Palazzo Comunale complex, this recently established museum has the largest collection (over 200 works) of Giorgio Morandi, Bologna's most famous contemporary artist (see box, p40). Morandi's gentle simplicity, mellow colours and his more mundane subjects may provide a refreshing change from the classical art and religious imagery prevalent in the city. The museum also contains a reconstruction of the artist's studio at via Fondazza 36, providing an insight into his work and methods.

Palazzo Podesta and Palazzo Re Enzo

piazza Maggiore. *Closed to public except during exhibitions.* *Map 4, C3-D3, p256*

The castle-like construction in the centre of piazza Maggiore in fact combines two buildings, the Palazzo Podesta and the Palazzo Re Enzo. Before becoming the governor's residence, the **Palazzo Podesta** was originally designed in the early 13th century to house the city's law court. Of the original structure only the Arengo tower, built in 1212, remains. The belfry with its *campanazzo* (literally 'bloody great bell' – it weighs 4700kg) was added in 1453 and the building's current form was the result of Giovanni II of the then ruling Bentivoglio dynasty who took a keen interest in embellishing the city and commissioned the architect Aristotele

Giorgio Morandi (1890-1964)

Morandi was born in Bologna and spent most of his life painting there or in the village of Vergato, 7 km from the city. His landscapes have been compared to the work of Cezanne for the recurring presence of similarly angular shapes and soft hues. Painting during a period of immense social upheaval, technological innovation and artistic explosion, he was initially drawn towards the work of the Futurists and Cubists. But ultimately he found his peace in more metaphysical painting, aligning himself with the artists Carra and De Chirico. He became the artist of simple everyday things: vases, fruit, windows, discovering them as if for the first time, revealing their hidden depths, and imbuing them with an existential significance. He once said, "Every thing is a mystery, ourselves and the most simple, most infinitesimal of things."

Fioravanti to renovate and redesign it. Particularly notable are the terracotta statues by Alfonso Lombardi on the pillars that support the tower, representing the city's patron saints, and the bas-reliefs of different animals which decorate the columns of the portico.

● *At the junction of the four passages at the foot of the belfry under the Palazzo Podesta, if you stand facing the wall and whisper, anyone standing diametrically opposite and facing the wall can hear what you are saying (traffic permitting). It is said that cheating lovers used to meet here to exchange sweet-nothings without fear of being discovered.*

Built in 1244 as an extra wing of the Palazzo del Podesta for civic functions the **Palazzo Re Enzo** takes its name from the man who was its prisoner for 22 years. Enzo, the blonde young king of Sardinia, was the illegitimate son of Frederick the Great, ruler of the occupying imperial army in the early 13th century. In 1249 the Papal Guelf forces won a historic victory over Frederick at the battle of nearby Fossalta and took his son prisoner. He was detained in this building until his untimely death there in 1271. The building became known as Enzo's *dorata prigione* (golden prison) on account of the luxury in which he was kept, complete with cooks, maids and courtiers to keep him entertained. The palazzo was restored at the beginning of the 20th century, salvaging the beautiful wooden vaulted staircase that leads up to various assembly rooms nowadays used for exhibitions and meetings.

● *Back when the main piazza was also used for executions, the executioner's wife, Lazzarina, kept flower pots next to the bodies of the hanged criminals displayed on the iron balustrade of the Palazzo Podestà. The expression "to end up in Lazzarina's garden" (the equivalent of "sleeping with the fishes") entered popular local parlance, although it has since fallen into disuse.*

Palazzo dei Notai

piazza Maggiore. *Mon and Wed 0900-1300, Tue, Thu and Fri 1500-1900. Map 4, D3, p256*

Nestled between the basilica and town hall is the Hall of the Notaries. With its more modest proportions and Gothic windows with their triforas and marble columns, it is more ornate and pleasing to the eye than the monsters which sandwich it. The oldest part of the building opposite the town hall dates back to the 13th century while the rest was added in the late 15th century. The building was the seat of the city Guild of Notaries and place of study for some of the legal scholars at Bologna's university who pioneered many of the basic principles of European law.

Palazzo dei Banchi

piazza Maggiore. *Closed to the public. Map 4, D4, p256*

Completing the enclosure of the square on its eastern side the Bankers' House (1412) is so named after the bankers and money lenders who use to have *banchi* ('benches' or stalls) under its arcades (indeed this is the origin of our word 'bank'). Originally a row of jumbled buildings they were brought together in the 16th century by the architect Vignola to create the present harmonious façade that is oddly classical compared to many of Bologna's old buildings. It is possible the façade also served to hide from the eyes of the medieval nobles the sore of the lower classes and small-time tradesmen with their businesses that populated the group of narrow streets immediately behind it known as the Quadrilatero. The majestic row of arcades underneath the façade is known as *il Pavaglione*. In the days when the piazza was used as a weekly market, this area was where the cocoons of the *pava* (silkworm) were sold under a large protective marquee or pavilion.

★ Il Quadrilatero and il Mercato di Mezzo
Map 4, D4-D5, p256

Il Quadrilatero is the name given to the grid of narrow streets hidden behind the east of piazza Maggiore. These streets were home to the small businessmen of medieval Bologna and each street still bears the name of the powerful associations of artisans and merchants it was known for: *orefici* (jewellers), *clavature* (locksmith), *pescherie* (fishmongers), *drapperie* (textile merchants). The grid, itself part of the original Roman settlement, used to extend further north but the roads were flattened to make way for via Rizzoli and piazza Ravegnana in line with the 19th-century fashion for boulevards. Today these are still among Bologna's liveliest market streets. By day they are full of the smells, colours and cries of butchers, grocers and the fresh local produce that makes the cuisine of this city so rich. By night they become the stage for Bologna's beautiful youth as they strut in and out of the many bars that have become some of the city's trendiest early evening nightspots.

Santuario di Santa Maria della Vita

via Clavature 10, **T** 051-236245, *0700-1300. Map 4, D4, p256*

You could be forgiven for missing this tiny church amid the bustle of the market streets of the Quadrilatero and its presence in such a hive of trade seems incongruous. Originally built in the late 17th century to house the ill and impoverished folk of this quarter the church grew a dome and became home to one of the unrivalled works of beauty in Bologna's treasure chest of fine art: the dramatic *Three Marys Lament over the Dead Christ*, by the sculptor Niccolo dell'Arca. Mary's desperation was once described by the poet Gabriele d'Annunzio as "a petrified scream". The next door oratory houses a famous group of 14 similarly expressive terracotta statues by Alfonso Lombardi called *Death of the Virgin*. These sculptures, realistic in their portrayal of human suffering, were in their time considered unworthy of note compared to the fashion for more idealized renderings of the narrative.

Palazzo dell'Archiginnasio

via dell'Archiginnasio. *Mon-Fri 0900-1800, Sat 0900-1330.*
Map 4, F4, p253

This rose-coloured building on the eastern flank of piazza Galvani, with its beautiful 139 m-long portico, was the seat of Bologna's university from 1563 until 1803 when it was transferred to via Zamboni. The idea, conceived by a professor of law named Pier Donato Ceri, was to bring together under one roof the various faculties of the university which had, since the 11th century, cropped up in a disordered way around the city.

The beautiful interior courtyard with its double loggia is also noted for the 6000 or so heraldic shields emblazoned under the arches. These shields replaced tower-buildings as the fashion by which noblemen, eminent professors, students and rich people could immortalize their families. Such was the rush for wall space,

Bologna

shields were disfigured by competing families leading to a law being passed to prevent such profanation.

The site is divided into two halves representing two basic distinctions in the realm of study that were made by the university, the southern half for Law and the northern half for students of the Arts (including mathematics and natural sciences). Under the loggia in the main courtyard is the Santa Maria dei Bulgari chapel which has some remnants of frescoes by Bartolomeo Ceso.

Within the Archiginnasio complex lies the **Teatro Anatomico** (*Mon-Sat 0900-1300, Mon-Fri 1300-1830)*, the beautiful dissection theatre made entirely out of wood and resembling a law court with delicately écorché wood statues of skinned torsos by Giannotti. Built in 1637 it is a replica of the original 1595 room where the importance of human dissection to medicine was first demon-strated, often to mass audiences. Dissections were only carried out in the winter months as Zanussi had not yet invented the fridge.

The Archiginnasio also houses the **Biblioteca Comunale** (municipal library), located here since 1838 and containing over 700,000 books and a collection of rare manuscripts that make it one of the most important libraries in Italy. The whole building suffered badly in a bombing raid in January 1944 but was skillfully restored to its current state.

Museo Civico Archeologico
via dell'Archiginnasio 2, **T** 051-233849. *Tue-Fri 0900-1800, Sun 1000-1830, Closed Mon. €4.13, concessions €2.07, under-14s free . Map 4, E4, p256*

This 14th-century building, itself a section of the Pavaglione, was formerly the Ospedale di Santa Maria della Morte, a hospital for the terminally ill and criminals sentenced to death. In the 16th century it underwent refurbishment before in 1881 becoming the home of the museum of municipal archaeology. Local archaeology might be a bit of a niche interest to the average visitor and the museum does have a rather stuffy atmosphere. That said, there is a rich collection of Egyptian artefacts and bas-reliefs (second in Italy only to the collection in Turin), various Greek and Roman antiquities including a bust of Emperor Nero, and an important collection of relics from the Etruscan civilization that made Bologna (or Felsina as they named it) the capital of northern Etruria and one of their most important economic centres from around the 5th century BC.

Metropolitana di San Pietro
Via dell'Indipendenza 7, **T** 051-222112. *0700-1200, 1530-1900 daily. Map 4, B4, p256*

Bologna's squat cathedral sits flush with one of the city's busiest streets like a plump bishop. As a result it feels rather shut in and, unlike its publicly funded rival, San Petronio, does not benefit from any space which would make it possible really to admire its façade or which might enable it to dominate or inspire awe in humble and fearful citizens in the way it was intended. That said, the two 13th-century lions in Veronese marble by Mastro Ventura that guard its entrance are magnificent and the vast interior conceals a number of beautiful terracotta figures and frescoes by hands of the Bolognese school, most notably the *Annunciation* by Ludovico Carracci in the sacristy. The 12th-century belfry by Mastro Alberto is also considered a masterpiece. Otherwise the overall building is a composite of ruins and refurbishments made to the original 9th-century Holy Roman church site that has suffered fires and earthquakes down the ages. Only a beautiful spiral column inside supported by the statue of a crossed legged man remains from its former elegance. Every year in May the image of Bolognese saint *la Madonna di San Luca* is brought down here from her sanctuary on the hill (see Festivals, p193).

● *Turning out of the church and left into via Altabella you find the remains of an arch known as the porta dei laureati (gate of the graduates) through which new graduates once passed.*

★ Il Quadrilatero
The ancient streets of the Quadrilatero open out onto piazza Maggiore

Chiesa e Convento di San Salvatore

via Volto Santo 1, **T** 051-222852. *0730-1200, 1500-1900.*
Map 4, D1, p256

Constructed in the 17th century, this church is unusual in Bologna
for its single nave and the echoes of Roman classicism in both the
exterior and interior. Many important pictures are to be found in
the various chapels inside, most notably perhaps the *Crowning of
the Virgin* by Vitale da Bologna. The figure of Thomas Becket, one
of the university's famous alumni, appears in the *Presentation of the
Virgin and of Saint Thomas of Canterbury* by Girolamo de Treviso.
This church also houses the tomb of *Il Guercino*, Giovani Francesco
Barbieri, one of the greatest Italian painters of the 17th century.
The associated 16th-century Augustine convent with its three
cloisters of double loggias and delicate columns is an impressive
monument for its deceptive size alone.

Piazza Roosevelt

Map 4, C1-D2, p256

As its name suggests this square to the west of piazza Maggiore
belongs to a more recent period in Bologna's history and was in
fact built on the ruins that ensued from the Allied bombardments
in 1943. Unattributed holes from shrapnel are still visible on the
walls opposite the Palazzo Comunale.

Palazzo Caprara

via IV Novembre 24. *Map 4, C-D1, p256*

Not many police forces nowadays can boast an HQ as beautiful as
this early 17th-century former nobleman's palace. It was commissioned by Carlo Caprara who went by the title Master of the Horse
of the Emperor and had inflated views of his station and what
residence would best reflect it. He couldn't keep up repayments

and had to sell, subsequent occupants gradually relieving it of its art heritage. Only the façade hints at its former splendour.

Palazzo Marescalchi
via IV Novembre 5. *Map 4, D1-2, p256*

Another of Bologna's majestic 17th-century noble houses, this palazzo is noted for its more than usually intricate exterior embellishments. Also impressive is the art on display in its drawing room, most notably the *Allegory of Air and Fire* by Guido Reni and a host of other decorations by other Bolognese hands.

Biblioteca Multimediale Sala Borsa
Piazza Nettuno 3, **T** 051-204400. *Map 4, C3, p256*

Alongside the Palazzo Comunale and near the old city mint in *via della Zecca* (road of the mint) is Bologna's former stock exchange. This is Bologna's only art-deco building, complete with stained-glass roof and cast-iron columns. It was commissioned in 1883 as a stock exchange but fell into disuse in 1903 due to lack of trade. In 1989 remains of the Roman forum were uncovered beneath the floor, visible through a glass floor. It is now the pride of Bologna's contemporary urban development plans – a multimedia exhibition hall and library, boasting some 270 networked computers containing all sorts of documentation on contemporary culture and Bologna's history. The library is particularly well-equipped for children.

Northeast: the university quarter

Shadowy porticoed streets that conceal buzzing and experimental cafés, bars, canteens by day and fine restaurants and underground clubs by night, mostly designed to suit the student pocket.
    *Heralded by the city's famous **Due Torri** (two towers) at its head,*

*the main artery of university life is **via Zamboni**, along which are to be found the university's faculty buildings and the bars in which the students spend their time 'revising'. Halfway along, **piazza Verdi** is the veritable heart of studentland, and also theatreland, while at the other end at the confluence with via delle Belle Arti is the famous **Pinacoteca** art museum.*

*Heading instead due north from via Rizzoli the atmosphere changes from the mystery of the winding medina-like alleys of the old **ghetto Ebraico** (Jewish ghetto), to the refined air of the boutiques of **via Oberdan** and beyond them the less-visited working-class back streets that conceal Bologna's ancient system of waterways on **via delle Moline** and **via Piella**. To the west, just off the via dell'Indipendenza is the city's cathedral of **San Pietro** while further north the streets open out into **piazza VIII Agosto**, stage of the city's bustling weekend market. Returning to the two towers and heading directly east the more sedate and tranquil **via San Vitale** is home to old noble residences and an abundance of antique and craft shops.*

▶▶ *See Sleeping p123, Eating and drinking p141, Bars and clubs p173*

◉ Sights

★ La Torre degli Asinelli and La Torre Garisenda
La Torre degli Asinelli 0900-1900, €3 . Map 4, C5, p256

Known colloquially as *Le Due Torri*, Bologna's twin towers have become the city's most immediately recognizable icon, its Leaning Tower of Pisa. Yet despite their apparent solitude on the city's skyline there used to be many more towers. In the 12th and 13th centuries any self-respecting Bolognese noble family had a tower and so intense was this practice of keeping *up* with the Joneses, or not wanting to be vertically challenged by your neighbour, that at the peak of their construction Bologna's cityscape boasted over a hundred towers. In this time the city was known affectionately as *la turrita* (the towered one) and must have looked, as observed the

English traveler, H V Morton, "like a bed of asparagus." It was in the urban regeneration program of 1889 that the engineer Giuseppe Ceri campaigned vociferously for Bologna's "old and useless" towers to be pulled down. The aberration was approved, proving that the 20th century did not have a monopoly on bad architectural taste, and the *Due Torri* are two of only a few towers of any significant height that survive. These early skyscrapers served as watch-towers to warn against an attack on the city and as a place of refuge should such an attack penetrate the city. In the 14th century they also had a brief role as a prison. Nowadays, beyond being a tourist attraction, the *due torri* serve as reception masts, a use of which Marconi, the Bolognese inventor of radio, would surely have approved.

At a height of nearly 98 m, La Torre degli Asinelli is the taller of the two, commissioned in the early 12th century by the powerful Asinelli family from which it takes its name. There are 498 sturdy oak steps leading to the top, twisting like an Escher fantasy around the inside wall which is otherwise hollow and providing for many cosy trysts on the way up and down. Smog permitting, the reward at the top is a stunning view over the city's rooftops and Bologna's guardian angel, the Basilica di San Luca to the southwest, and which on a clear day can stretch as far as the Adriatic to the east and the Alps to the north.

Built almost simultaneously, the leaning Torre Garisenda (*closed to the public*), was originally much higher than its current 47.5 m. It started to lurch through subsidence in the mid 1300s and was truncated from its original 77 m for fear that it might topple. One urban myth has it that the tower was built at an angle as an alternative in the tower-vanity stakes. Romantic legend has it that one of the young Garisenda noblemen was in love with a fair Asinelli maiden and asked that the tower be built like this so that he could touch his beloved's hair. Taking a leaf out of his own book, the hedonistic French poet Theophile Gauthier, likened the two towers to two mates stumbling home and leaning on each other, drunk.

Of Guelphs and Ghibellines

The conflict between the Guelphs and the Ghibellines was a major feature of 13th-century Italy. The Guelphs were followers of the Pope and the Ghibellines supporters of the Emperor, Frederick the Great and alliances for each side divided the country's many controlling family dynasties. In Bologna the two families to whom the conflicting factions allied themselves were, on one side, the Geremei, who were Guelfs and on the other the Lambertazzi family who were Ghibellines.

Following their victory at the battle of Fossalta in 1249, the Guelfs took control of the city and submitted it to the control of Pope Nicholas III who from 1278 ruled the city by proxy from Rome. However, despite this yoke Bologna was always allowed to enjoy relative autonomy for fear of further insurrection.

Bologna's buildings tell of a history of oscillation between Papal and Imperial forces, its buildings usually being conceived as statements of preeminence of one over the other or altered by a new incumbent in deliberate architectural snubs.

Perhaps the most famous example of the Guelf-Ghibelline conflict lies further north in Verona where at the same time as the battle of Fossalta two young lovers were trying to transcend their families' different allegiances. Their names were Romeo and Juliet.

Bologna

● *At the foot of the Garisenda tower you can see an inscription quoting the reference made to the tower in Canto XXXI of the Inferno of Dante's Divina Commedia, where the poet uses it as a simile for the looming giant, Antaeus.*

51

Chiesa di San Bartolomeo

piazza di Porta Ravegnana. *0700-1300, 1500-1630.*
Map 4, D6, p256

Just behind the two towers this small church, whose reconstruction in the 16th century was left unfinished, contains some
lovely frescoes, particularly the *San Carlo al sepolcro di Varallo* by
Ludovico Carracci in the second right-hand chapel and Guido
Reni's *Vergine col Putto* in the eighth.

Ghetto Ebraico

Map 4, B5-6, p256

Diving just behind the contemporary via Rizzoli the atmosphere
changes and the alleyways take on a mysterious, secretive and
labyrinthine aspect more resonant of an Arabian medina. Hemmed
in by via Goito and full of evocatively named streets such as via
dell'Inferno (Hell Street) this was formely Bologna's Jewish Ghetto.
Although it is thought that the Jewish community was allowed to
contribute much to Bologna's cultural beginnings in the 12th century, in the 1500s they were, as in many cities, ghettoized, and
forced to live in this confined area in constant fear of persecution.
To guard against attack they built spy-holes into their doors, which
are still visible, for example at via Inferno 3 and via Valdonica 14.
Nowadays the ghetto is still attractively dark and mysterious but
long-since secularized and home to a number of good restaurants.
The ghetto and surrounding areas also contain many curious
buildings such as la **Chiesa di San Giobbe**, a former church subsequently used as a hospital for sufferers of *mal francese* (literally
'French evil' or syphilis) and now subsumed within a pleasant
shopping mall called the **Galleria Acquaderni** whose shops still
bear the church's frescoes on some of their walls. Here are also to
be found a number of the city's other surviving towers: the **Torre
degli Uguzzoni** in vicolo Tubertini, the 11th-century **Torre**

Prendiparte (59 m) in via Sant'Alo, also known as *la coronata* (crowned one) on account of its crenellations, the **Casa-torre Guidozagni**, near via Albriroli which was lowered in 1487 to its current height, and the **Torre degli Azzoguidi**, also known as *l'Altabella*, reputedly after a tall and fair Bolognese lady of the quarter, on via Caduti di Cefalonia.

Palazzo Malvezzi and Palazzo Magnani
Palazzo Malvezzi, via Zamboni 13; Palazzo Magnani, via Zamboni 20. *Map 4, C7, p256*

At the top of via Zamboni are a clutch of fine noble houses now variously the seat of banks and local government. The **Palazzo Malvezzi** is known for its grandiose staircase by Francesco Bibiena and the fine statue of Hercules, complete with club and lion at its entrance. Palazzo Magnani contains in its first floor drawing room arguably one of Bologna's finest art treasures, a cycle of 14 hectic and wonderfully animated and fantastical frescoes by Annibale Carracci, completed between 1588-91, depicting the foundation of Rome, complete with satyrs, hermaphrodites and masks.

★ Chiesa di San Giacomo Maggiore
via Zamboni/piazza Rossini, **T** 051-225970. *Mon-Sun 0600-1200, 1530-1800. Map 4, B8, p256*

As with many of Bologna's churches, San Giacomo has undergone several additions and restructures over the centuries so that little is left of its Venetian-Gothic origins and it appears as a bit of a mish-mash of styles. Originally built in the mid-13th century the church was appropriated in the 15th century by the Bentivoglio family who made this area of the city their power base and whose wish most of the revisions were. Perhaps the most striking of these is the beautiful pink side arcade. The recurring motif on the capitals is the seashell, symbol of the traveller and pilgrim San Giacomo

(St James). The apse of the church still supports remains of the second circle of the old city wall. Within San Giacomo's Renaissance interior the church houses many artistic treasures, most notable of which are *Saint Roch* by Ludovico Carracci, the tomb of Galeazzo Bentivoglio by Jacopo della Quercia and the Bentivoglio's own private chapel, the altar of which has some striking artwork by Lorenzo Costa depicting family victories over other Bolognese dynasties. The *Madonna Enthroned, Thanked by Giovanni II and his Wife Ginevra Sforza and their Children* is the eloquent and literal title of a painting by Lorenzo Costa specially commissioned by Giovanni II, the family Godfather, as a votive offering to thank the Almighty for their escape from an attempted massacre by the Malvezzi family. Other than by building towers, it was also fashionable to show your power by buying and decorating your own chapel. Costa's two paintings to the left of the above were the painter's ironic way of showing how hollow earthly fame becomes in death.

Oratorio di Santa Cecilia

via Zamboni 15 (entrance through portico Bentivolgio next to San Giacomo Maggiore). *1000-1300, 1500-1900 daily, free.*
Map 4, C8, p256

A great patron of the arts, the Bentivoglio Lord, Giovanni II, ruling Bologna at the beginning of the 16th century, commissioned a large number of projects to embellish his city. Among them were the frescoes depicting the life of Santa Cecilia in this little oratory through the archway of San Giacomo which were painted by some of the greatest artists living in the city at that time: Francesco Francia, Lorenzo Costa and Amico Aspertini. Recently restored and opened to the public with new lighting, this is one of Bologna's real art treasures.

● *Above the arch leading into via del Carro beyond San Giacomo Maggiore is a mask from which wine flowed onto the crowd below on festive occasions.*

Teatro Comunale

via Zamboni 30/Large Respighi 1, **T** 051-529011/529999,
www.comunalebologna.it   *Map 4, B8, p256*

Map 4, B8, p256

Bologna's city theatre was built in the 18th century on the site of
part (the stables) of the magnificent palace of the Bentivoglio
family which was razed to the ground when that dynasty was overthrown in 1507. It was designed by Antonio Bibiena, a member of
the renowned Galli family of Italian theatre designers. The colos-
seum-like 'boxes' and the u-shaped arena were a favoured form at
the time. The theatre opened in 1763 with a performance of
Gluck's *Triumph of Clelia*. Guided tours in Italian and English take
place on Sundays at 1000 and Mondays at 1100. Tours last around
one hour and cost €7 per person. **T** 0347-3335791.

Conservatorio di Musica G B Martini and Museo Bibliografico Musicale

piazza Rossini 2, **T** 051-222997/221117. *0900-1300. Closed Sun.
Entry free.*   *Map 4, C7, p256*

Map 4, C7, p256

Bologna played host to many famous Italian composers such as
Verdi, Rossini and Puccini and its music conservatory was a place of
study and composition for many others, among them Bellini, Gluck,
Wagner and, briefly, Mozart. Just off piazza Rossini, the building is a
former Augustine convent confiscated, like many, by Napoleon
and put to other use. It is easy to see how the cloistered setting
might have provided inspiration. The magnificent concert hall has
a huge organ and a gallery of portraits of great composers, musicians and divas of bygone days. More important is the collection of
autographed scripts and rare scores from the 16th to 18th centuries, including the original of *The Barber of Seville*, kept in the Liceo
Musicale. There are also hundreds of portraits of JC Bach by
Gainsborough, a portrait of Farinelli (a famous castrato) by Giaquinto
and a beautiful canvas entitled *A Musical Library* by Giuseppe Crespi.

Musei di Palazzo Poggi

via Zamboni 31-33, **T** 051-259021/2099360. *Mon-Fri 0830-1730, Sat-Sun 0900-1830 for all museums. All free.* *Map 2, H11, p253*

The seat of Europe's oldest university was originally located in the Archiginnasio but was moved here in 1803 by Napoleon who wanted to bring all the city's proliferating faculties together in one place to create a kind of campus. This is the engine room of Bologna *la dotta* (Bologna the learned), the home of the university library and many of the university's main faculties and museums. The 16th-century building was the former home of the Poggi family who, although of humble origin, wished it to be built at the cost of almost the entire family wealth, to signify the family's social ascent with the making of one of their number a cardinal.

The Palazzo Poggi houses a series of diverse museums reflecting the vast range of subjects that were pioneered at the university by its early pupils.

L'Accademia della Scienza is the university's science institute, whose lower rooms are decorated in frescoes representing Ulysses by Pellgrino Tibaldi. The entrance at number 33 leads into a pleasant courtyard with a statue to Hercules in its centre by Angelo Pio. The Aula Carducci is the hall preserved in the state when Bologna's famous poet gave his lectures there between 1860 and 1904.

Atop the Palazzo Poggi and accounting for its rather odd shape is **La Specola dell'Osservatorio Astronomico** and **Museo di Astronomia**, a tower which houses the university's observatory and museum of astronomy, full of all sorts of ancient instruments for the measuring and examination of the skies, evocative and fascinating for their rather Heath-Robinsonesque appearance.

! Many cities claim to have the oldest university in the world but Bologna has a better claim than most. It certainly pre-dates Oxford, Cambridge and Spanish competitors – why else would the Spanish have come to Bologna in such droves?

Bologna's arcades

Some enterprising person has calculated that there are 44 km of arcades in Bologna, including those leading up to San Luca but not the modern attempts in rebuilt areas such as via Marconi in the north west. The longest distance you can cover without emerging from underneath an arcade is the 8 km from the chiesa degli Alemanni near porta Maggiore up to San Luca. Arcades are the city's leitmotif loved by all for the changing perspectives and the tranquility they afford. The first arcades are thought to have been built around the year 1000 to accomodate the city's expansion at the founding of the university and arrival of foreign students. Medieval additions sat precariously on top of houses with the support of wooden braces. Arcades were a practical solution for providing adequate support, increasing space above and providing shelter for pedestrians and merchants below. A law was passed making the minimum height seven feet so that people on horseback could pass under them. The symmetry of their design also fitted with the classical and humanist ideas of proportion and harmony being championed in the architecture of the time.

Although it may seem strange for a landlocked city the **Museo delle Navi**, Bologna's maritime museum, is considered to be one of the most important in the world for its rare models of 17th- and 18th-century warships which fascinated studying scientists for their technological innovation and advancement.

The **Museo di Architettura Militare** places military developments in the context of scientific and technological advancements. Models of various forms of armament and toy soldiers are on display, plus early defence diagrams carved in beautiful marquetry.

Finally and not necessarily uppermost in the average visitor's mind the **Museo Ostretrico Giovanni Antonio Galli**, the university's obstetrics museum, has a wide range of 18th-century instruments and incredible life-size models by Galli in wax and wood demonstrating the different phases of pregnancy in order to prepare 18th-century midwives for every eventuality.

There are many other small museums of niche interest within Palazzo Poggi. Behind Palazzo Poggi, along the roads of largo Trombetti, via Belmeloro and via Selmi, which are all part of the university in that many faculties and lecture rooms are found here, are still more museums for real enthusiasts of other very specific subjects not necessarily on the shopping list of the general visitor: comparative anatomy, anatomy of pets, and anthropology. The zoology museum is worth a look if you're into dead fish, birds, sea-shells and want to see a stuffed rhinoceros. A complete list of these museums can be found in the museums listing (p101).

● *The poet Dante Alighieri was one of Bologna university's most illustrious students. He is known to have taken a keen interest in science and in particular in astronomy. It is thought that the structure and mechanics of his* Divina Commedia *are likely to have been inspired by his student years.*

Museo di Geologia e Paleontologia
via Zamboni 63, **T** 051-2099360. *Mon-Fri 0900-1230.*
Map 2, H12, p253

The university's other main collection of faculties and museums is across the road from Palazzo Poggi further down towards the decaying 13th-century gate of Porta San Donato. The best of these museums is Italy's largest museum of paleontology, containing over 1000 pieces, of which the most appealing (especially to children) will be one of only four existing examples in Europe of the friendly but enormous diplodocus dinosaur, 26 m long and 4 m tall. A full listing of other museums in this building can be found in the listing on p101.

Orto Botanico and l'Erbario
via Irnerio 42, **T** 051-351299. *Mon-Fri 0800-1500, l'Erbario,* **T** 051-351304. *Mon-Fri 8.30am-12.30pm, and* Palazzina della Viola, via Filippo Re. *Map 2, F11, p253*

After streets of constant and intensive museum-visiting the botanical gardens and herbarium make for a relaxing break. At two hectares this geometrically beautiful garden of soothing lawns is a favourite for lounging students hanging out between lectures. Founded in 1658, it is home to over 5000 species of local and exotic species of plant, while the Herbarium has specimens of over 110,000 dried plants. The adjoining **Palazzina della Viola**, named after the violets of Giovanni II Bentivoglio's gardens nearby is now the home of the university's faculty of agriculture.

Museo di Anatomia Umana
via Irnerio 48 **T** 051-276811. *Mon-Sat 0900-1200, free.* *Map 2, G12, p253*

On a leafy boulevard the museum of anatomy is Bologna's answer to Madame Tussauds, the difference being that the waxworks here were created not in the name of vanity but in the pursuit of scientific knowledge and, specifically, the practice of dissection, the body being far easier to understand "with the eyes than with the ears" as its founder, Pope Benedict XIV said. It is not necessarily the place you thought you'd end up on a visit to the city but the models, all hand sculpted as opposed to moulded, are of an exquisite accuracy and beauty, important in their own right as objects of art but also in demonstrating the services of art to science.

> ### Taddeo Pepoli
>
> Bologna's history is populated by individuals and families that at one time of other held sway over the city between periods of Papal rule and outside occupation. Taddeo Pepoli, a vicar by calling, dominated public life in the tumultuous years between 1337-1344 owing to his skill in the art of diplomacy between Guelf and Ghibellines. Other members of the Pepoli family continued to have great influence in the region until the end of the 18th century.

★ La Pinacoteca Nazionale

Via delle Belle Arti 56, **T** *051-243222. Tue-Sun, 0900-1900, closed Mon. Entry €4, €3 with museum card, concessions €2. Free for under 18s and over 60s. Map 2, G/H11, p253*

Bologna's National Gallery is a must for art-lovers and historians of art but also provides an insight into the important role Bologna played in the cultural development of Italy which can sometimes be obscured by the allure of other more famous art treasures elsewhere in the country. The gallery contains the largest collection of canvasses by artists from the influential 17th-century Bolognese school of painting, among them Tibaldi, Reni, the Carracci brothers, and Guercino, some late Titian, and also some masterpieces from preceding centuries including a polyptych by Giotto and *St George and the Dragon* by Vitale di Bologna. The gallery was founded by Napoleon as part of his programme for cultural reform and the collection based on a set of donations to Pope Clement VII. To this Napoloeon added all the art he was able to confiscate from the various churches, convents and monasteries he suppressed during his occupation. In so doing his vision was to unify the canvasses (now located in a suppressed Jesuit convent) with the Accademia delle Belle Arti next door – a logical union of the practice of art and examples of its perfection. Napoleon's reforms did not stop many of the works of art ending up in the Louvre, some of which have been returned.

Nuovo Palazzo Bentivoglio

via delle Belle Arti 8. *Closed to public except courtyard.*
Map 2, H9, p253

Having destroyed the magnificent Bentivoglio palace in 1507 it seems the citizens of Bologna repented their hasty overthrow of the dynasty who had held such power in the 15th century and whose patronage had embellished so much of their city. This imposing structure built in swift homage in the mid-16th century by Tibaldi is a suggestive reminder of their former hegemony even if today it is home to a few less lordly residents and small businesses. The unfinished courtyard exudes an atmosphere of neglect but it is worth a look for its beautiful Romanesque double loggias.

Chiesa di San Martino

via Oberdan 25. *0700-1300, 1500-1830. Map 4, A6, p256*

Stranded between the university district and via dell'Indipendenza this little church with its tranquil piazza is often ignored in favour of the city's bigger attractions. The recent discovery of a fragment of a fresco by Paolo Uccello depicting the Nativity in the first left-hand chapel may change this, although other masterpieces have been found inside, notably the *Adoration of the Magi* in the Boncompagni family chapel by Aspertini. Begun in the early 13th century, in the face of much resistance by the Augustine monks of San Giacomo nearby, this is one of few examples in Bologna of a church that has not been tampered with through the ages and remains much as it was, save for the 19th-century façade. The church used to be accessed by crossing a small bridge over a weir, which has since been covered up.

★ Palazzo Grassi

The original wooden form of Bologna's trademark porticoes can be seen at Palazzo Grassi.

Palazzo Grassi
via Marsala 12. *Closed to the public.* *Map 2, H8, p253*

With its Tudor-like wooden porticoes and beams, this is a rare and beautifully intact vestige of 13th-century Bologna and one of the city's oldest buildings. The wooden porticoes also remain on the buildings opposite making this a very picturesque little back-corner of the city.

Via delle Moline and Bologna's canals

Map 2, G8-H9, p253

Unlike most big cities Bologna was not built on a river and thus had to divert water from elsewhere. In the 12th century a canal was built to divert water from the westerly river Reno to the city centre. The water served not only for sanitation and refreshment but also, through the watermills after which via delle Moline is named, for power to fuel the silk and hemp industries that were Bologna's main medieval commercial activities. Up until the early 20th century the canal also served as a transportation vehicle for the import of essential goods to the city. The Reno is connected to the Po in the north enabling the transport of Veronese marble and other materials for the construction and embellishment of the city. The canal lock at Casalecchio west of Bologna used to be one of the city's most picturesque spots until suburban sprawl and modern transportation methods dictated that the canals fell into disuse and were covered over by roads. Although it may seem unlikely, water still flows through the foundations of old Bologna but it is still visible in only a few places, most notably the bridge on via Piella opposite which is a peep-hole into the watery past, and between via Capo di Lucca and via Alessandrini. This area has been ambitiously referred to as Bologna's Little Venice. The comparison is odious as this poor working class quarter has a seedy, medieval quality all of its own.

Piazza VIII Agosto

Map 2, F8, p253

Named after the battle in which the Bolognese repelled the attentions of the invading Austrians in the First War of Italian Independence in 1848, this square looks for five days a week like an ugly and anonymous car park at odds with the city's prevailing aesthetics. Also known as La Piazzola, on Fridays and Saturdays it turns into a huge and colourful market which draws locals and bargain hunters from the provinces in their droves. Wares on offer range from shoes, gloves and other leather goods to books, china and various household items. The simultaneous bric-a-brac market is up the steps in the Giardini della Montagnola.

Giardini Pubblici della Montagnola

Open all day, closed at night. Times vary according to season.
Map 2, E8, p253

For all its porticoes and cobbled streets Bologna can seem like a city of unrelenting stone, unsoothed by nature and open spaces. An aerial view shows that many of the city's green spaces are closed off from street-level view by the palazzi and courtyards which surround them. The public Montagnola Gardens represent the largest green space inside the Centro Storico. They were land-scaped by Giambattista Martinetti in 1806 on the mound created by the excavations and ruins of the papal castle, Castello di Galliera, of which a ruin still remains at their northern end. A grand set of steps leads up into the gardens at the foot of which is a dramatic and sensuous statue to Venus and Neptune by Diego Sarti. On Fridays and Saturdays the gardens host a vast flea-market popular with dedicated peddlers and idle browsers.

Via San Vitale

Map 3, A9-B12, p255

With its preponderance of expensive antique shops and galleries, via San Vitale is more sedate nowadays than the bohemian univer-sity hangouts of via Zamboni and via delle Belle Arti. In Roman times it was known as the *via Salaria* as it led out towards the salt mines at Cervia, beyond Ravenna. Consisting of one almost contin-uous portico on both sides, the road is lined with many fine palazzi open to the public, notably the **Palazzo Orsi** at number 28 which is full of interesting and dramatic Baroque statues and painted ceilings, and fortress-like **Palazzo Fantuzzi** with elephant motifs in its façade at number 23, which has a beautiful staircase lined with statues. At number 56 is the **Palazzo Scagliarini-Rossi**, 19th-century home of Cornelia Rossi, the beautiful wife of the landscape architect Martinetti who is said to have 'surrounded' herself with the intelligentsia and artists of the time, including Byron, and held legendary parties. The atmospheric road of **via Broccaindosso** was one of the homes of the poet Carducci at number 20.

Torresotto
At the midway point of via San Vitale. Map 3, A10, p255

This tower is a rare survivor of the 16 tower gates that were built in the late 12th century as Bologna's second ring of defence against Emperor Frederick I (Barbarossa). The crenellated wall ran for 4 km around the city with an average height of 8 m.

Chiesa di Santi Vitale e Agricola
via San Vitale 48. *0700-1300, 1500-1830.* Map 4, C8, p256

This is a Romanesque church to Bologna's first martyrs, the return of whose relics from the occupying Franks coincided closely with the foundation of the post-Roman city. It is most notable for the paintings in its chapel and a beautiful crypt. Vitale and Agricola are said to have been killed on this spot by the Emperor Diocletian during the Christian persecutions.

Southeast: Santo Stefano and around

*Though fed by the attractive capillaries of **via Santo Stefano** and **via Castiglione**, nowhere is the beauty of this area more evident than in the triangular **piazza Santo Stefano**, site of the intricate* *complex of churches of the same name, one of the great architectural and artistic wonders of the city. The important **strada Maggiore**, once part of the Roman via Emilia, witnessed the coming and going, the coronation and invasions of alternate patriarchs and popes. These left their mark on this quarter of the city in a dense forestation of statements. From luxurious palaces and gardens (sadly closed to the public) to exquisite churches and sanctuaries such as **Santa Maria dei Servi** and the **Basilica of Santo Domenico**, all are home to countless masterpieces of the decorative arts. Narrow and shadowy in contrast, via Castligione leads up to the murky backwater of the **Mirasoli** district whose dark, faceless streets still exude the stench of the suspicion that reigned many hundreds of years ago, now replaced by the cheer of some of the best ,but least-visited, restaurants in town.*

▸▸ *See Sleeping p126, Eating and drinking p147, Bars and clubs p177*

◉ Sights

Loggia della Mercanzia
piazza della Mercanzia. Access to entrance hall only
Map 4, D6, p256

Today housing the Chamber of Commerce, the late 14th-century former customs house designed by the architect di Vicenzo in the city's traditional red and white livery is one of the finest Gothic buildings in Bologna. Having suffered significant damage during the Allied bombardments, its florid windows and extravagant balcony, from which merchants' decisions were announced to the populus, have been lovingly restored. Also of note are the clock and the bulding's many niches full of statues to saints and symbols of civic justice.

● *To the right of the Loggia della Mercanzia is an inscription to make any modern-day student jealous. Roughly translated it states that in recognition of the importance of the city's university, students shall have free books, clothes and food.*

Palazzo Bolognini
via Santo Stefano 9-11. *Map 4, E6, p256*

Further up via Santo Stefano from the Loggia della Mercanzia is the former house of another of Bologna's powerful families, the Bolognini. Built in the 16th century the building is also known as the *palazzo delle teste* (the palace of heads) on account of the many clay busts that look down onto the street and which have been attributed to the sculptor Alfonso Lombardi.

Le Case Isolani and La Corte Isolani
Map 4, E6-7, p256

An elegant passageway links via Santo Stefano to the strada Maggiore via a series of courtyards which in the way they are decorated represent a journey from the Middle Ages to the Renaissance. At either end are two houses named after the merchants who plied Cypriot wares here in the 13th century (*isolani* literally means 'from the islands'). The house on the side of piazza Santo Stefano has a marvellous spiral staircase by Vignola leading up to rooms adorned with many fine paintings by 17th- and 18th-century Bolognese hands. The house on the Strada Maggiore side (no. 19) is characterized by a spectacular 10-m high wooden portico. Today the passageway in between is home to boutiques, banks, restaurants and cafés.

● *Under the portico of strada Maggiore 19, if you crane your neck and peer up in to the murky wooden darkness you can see two mysterious wooden arrows sticking into the ceiling. Much mythology surrounds the origins of these arrows (of which there were once three) but the most probable explanation is that they were put there in jest by builders restoring the portico in the 19th century when the two supporting pillars were added.*

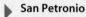

San Petronio

In the fifth century, during the decline of the Roman Empire, Bologna fell to ruin as all the political and administrative infrastructure disappeared. Petronius was a local bishop about whom little is known other than that he was a follower of Saint Ambrosius (patron saint of Milan) but whom legend has credited with rescuing the city by defining its boundaries and embarking upon the design and construction of a number of buildings, ensuring the city's continued protection and development. Most notable of the buildings he is thought to have conceived is the complex of interlinked churches of Santo Stefano, inspired by a similar design which Petronius brought back from a pilgrimage to Palestine and the Holy City. It was not until the Middle Ages, as Bologna with its university and resilient civic spirit became more distinct, that her citizens began to seek a symbol of their origins to which they could attach their identity. The result of their root-searching was to elevate their mysterious saviour-bishop to the status of patron saint.

Via Santo Stefano
Map 3, B8-G12, p255

Along via Santo Stefano are many fine noble houses, which conceal lovely courtyards behind their gates. The pavement is uneven in parts reputedly due to rich families wanting to distinguish their addresses from neighbours'. At number 31 is the old **Teatro Corso** inaugurated by Napoloeon and which witnessed the debut of the young composer, Gioacchino Rossini. At number 33 is the **Palazzo Finzi-Contini** which used to house the *albergo del Corso* where the romantic novelist Giacomo Leopardi stayed, a sojourn which inspired his novel *Nel Giardino dei Finzi-Contini*.

Piazza Santo Stefano
Map 4, E7, p256

Surrounded by intriguing and beautiful buildings, this piazza is one of Bologna's most picturesque locations. Triangular in shape, the cobbled square is also paved with lines of flat, grey stones, an aesthetic device in conflict with classical ideas of symmetry but intended when coming into the piazza from the north to lead the eye towards the church at the piazza's southern end.

★ Chiesa di Santo Stefano
via Santo Stefano 24, **T** 051-223256. *Mon-Sun 0900-1200, 1530-1830. Map 4, F7, p256*

Along with the Basilica of San Petronio and the Due Torri this church is one of the must-sees for any visitor to Bologna. At its peak it was a Russian doll of seven interlinked churches within churches. Its fifth-century circular core built around a natural spring was constructed by Bishop Petronius, soon-to-be patron saint of Bologna, on the site of a temple to the pagan goddess Isis. The complex is sometimes referred to as *La Santa Gerusalemme* after the seven connecting sanctuaries in the Holy City. Petronius is supposed to have brought back a copy of the similar design from a fifth-century trip to Palestine.

   The church is rumoured to be named after the Christian martyr St Stephen, whose remains were found in Jerusalem around the same time. Although the precise evolution of the building is not known, it is thought that the additions and expansions were added variously by the occupying Lombards, and then the Benedictine and Celestine monks between 983 and 1493. The complex was restored between 1870-1930. This also brought about some inexplicable demolitions which reduced the number of churches to the current four.

Le Brigate Rosse

The Red Brigades were a revolutionary left-wing movement that staged kidnappings and cold-blooded killings and terrorized the Italy of the late 1970s and early 1980s – a time which came to be known as the *anni di piombo* (years of lead). The culmination of their activity was the kidnapping and murder in 1978 of the former Prime Minister, Aldo Moro of the centre-right Christian Democrat Party. The terrorist group was formed in 1969 by armed students who wanted Italy to withdraw from NATO and become a Marxist-Leninist state. Through their activity they inevitably made enemies that formed mirror groups in the far-right wing, such as the fascist *Ordine Nuovo*. Political terrorism was thought to have vanished from Italy until March 21st 2002, when Marco Biagi was murdered outside his home in Bologna. Biagi was advising Italy's current Prime Minister, Silvio Berlusconi on controversial changes to employment law. The attack is thought to have been the work of a Red Brigade splinter-group in protest at what is perceived by many less extreme Italians to be Berlusconi's monopolistic control of the media and neo-fascist tendencies.

The first and principal church is the **Chiesa del Santissimo Crocefisso** to which the restorations returned its Lombardic medieval aspect. The beautiful crypt is composed of columns, capitals and other materials from the original Roman construction and bears a pagan inscription to Isis.

The **Basilica dei Santi Vitale e Agricola** is thought to be Bologna's oldest Christian church, again built from the original pagan construction with 11th-century Lombardic naves, and housing the sarcopoghi of the two martyrs of Bologna from which it takes its name. The tranquil *cortile di Pilato* is named after the

Lombardic facsimile of Pontius Pilate's bowl in its centre (where he 'washed his hands' of Christ).

To the north is the **Chiesa del San Sepolcro** (*closed 1200-1530*) which contains the bones of Saint Petronius (except the skull which is in the basilica). Note a charming image of an angel atop the empty tomb of Christ with dozing soldiers and the women who discovered Christ's disappearance. At Easter the sepulchre is opened to allow people in to recreate the discovery of the Resurrection.

To the west is the **Chiesa della Trinita**, virtually unrecognisable as a church after the restorations but housing a beautiful fresco of the *Adoration of the Magi* by Simone de' Crocefissi. Beyond this is the peaceful Romanesque cloister with a beautifully harmonious double loggia supported by capitals playfully decorated with sculpted animals, built by the Benedictines in the 11th century. A small **museum** contains various works of art recovered during the restoration works showing the evolution of Bolognese and Italian painting, most notably the 13th-century *Massacre of the Innocents* in the left-hand room.

★ Chiesa di Santa Maria dei Servi
strada Maggiore, **T** 051-226807. *0700-1145, 1545-1945.*
Map 3, C10-11, p255

Despite the rude intrusion of nearby traffic one cannot fail to be affected by the delicacy and fragility of the quadriportico (four-sided arcade) that stands before this church. There was originally only one side arcade, built in 1393. The completion of the square was one of the few beautiful interventions of the 19th century although it came at the cost of demolishing the church of San Tommaso which had for hundreds of years stood in its centre. Inside, the church is no less special and is best known as the site of a *Madonna and Child* by Cimabue and some 14th-century frescoes by Lippo di Dalmasio and Vitale da Bologna, although these should not obscure the many 17th- and 18th-century Bolognese-school paintings which are mostly to be found in the sacristy and convent. At Christmas time the Santa Lucia fair, with Nativity figures, Christmas tree and toys, is held in the quadrangle.

Chiesa di San Giovanni in Monte
via Monticelli. *Mon-Sun 0800-1200, 1500-1800.* *Map 3, C9, p255*

More of a gallery than a church, this raised 13th-century building with a 15th-century Venetian façade contains a stunning collection of paintings within its Gothic interior, including works by Guercino, Francesco del Cossa and the Crowning of the Virgin altarpiece by Lorenzo Costa. In the middle of the central nave is the bizarre sight of an upturned old Roman Corinthian column topped by a cross in a symbol of Christianity's victory over paganism. The majestic terracotta eagle, symbol of St. John in the lunetta above the wooden door is by Nicolo dell'Arca.

Piazza San Domenico
Map 3, D7, p255

This peaceful square laid with river pebbles has a distinct rural feel and also serves as a showcase to a number of important monuments such as the 14th-century elevated tomb to Rolandino de' Passegeri, one of the city's Notaries and a founding father of European law and human rights who is remembered for his heroic resistance to Frederick II in the name of freedom and democracy. The piazza's two columns support statues to the Virgin in celebration of the end of the plague in 1632 and to San Domenico, the latter being sculpted according to a drawing by Guido Reni.

★ Chiesa di San Domenico

piazza San Domenico. **T** 051-6400411. *Daily 0700-1300, 1430-2000. Map 3. D7/8, p255*

Begun in 1221 to commemorate the life of Domingo de Guzman, the founder of the Dominican order, this church contains one of the masterpieces of Bolognese heritage, the Fabergé-esque *arca* or canopy to the tomb of the saint in the right-hand nave, designed by Nicola Pisano and executed by Niccolo de Bari, the beauty of which earned him the name Niccolo dell'Arca. He died before all the statuettes had been completed, leaving the outstanding work – the figures of Saint Petronious and Saint Procolus – to no less a hand than Michelangelo. Among the bas-reliefs on the ark is a little dog. Legend has it that before his birth, Domenico's mother had a vision that she would give birth to a dog that would spread light and happiness in the name of the Lord. As with many of the city's churches, additions were made in the form of lavish side chapels to the vanity of various ruling families, decorated with superb fres-coes by Ludovico Carracci, di Dalmasio, Filippino Lippi (*The Mystic Marriage of St Catherine*), Guido Reni (*The Glory of Saint Dominic*) and other masters of the Bolognese school. Guido Reni is buried in the Rosario chapel in the church. The nearby convent is composed of two cloisters, the first, the cloister dei Morti (of the Dead) noted for its Roman-Gothic belltower, and the other for being the cell, home and deathbed of the saint himself. There is also a small **museum** beyond the apse of the main basilica (*Tue-Sun, 1000-1200, 1500-1800, free*).

Conservatorio and Chiesa della Madonna del Baraccano

piazza del Barracano 2, **T** 051-392680. *Sat-Sun 1000-1300, 1600-1900. Map 3, F11, p255*

Set into the remains of the third and outer circle of the old city walls this church is famous for the 15th-century portico through which it is accessed. The building above the portico is the seat of the Conservatorio del Baraccano, which was established in 1531 as a kind of finishing school for less well-off young girls. The church itself was commissioned by Giovanni Bentivoglio in 1472 to subsume a small chapel that bears an image of the Madonna set in the city walls. Ever preoccupied with beauty, various additions including the cupola were made in the 15th and 16th centuries to enhance the overall aesthetic effect.

Strada Maggiore
Map 3, B9-C12, p255

This important street, a suburban section of the Roman via Emilia, is lined with a series of former noble residences. At number 24 the *casa Sampieri* has paintings by all three Carraccis in the three ground floor rooms with ceilings by Guercino. At number 44 the imposing *palazzo Bargellini* is recognisable by the enormous, sinuous and muscular statues of Atlas that stand on either side of the entrance supporting the balcony above (the Greek god Zeus condemned Atlas to support the weight of the world on his shoulders for having colluded with the Titans' plot to overthrow him). This building houses the **Davia Bargellini** fine-art collection (*T 051-236708, Tue-Sun 0900-1400, free*) which includes many famous masterpieces from the 14th through to the 18th century by both Crespis and Donato Creti. Art pilgrims will not want to miss the *Madonna and Child* and deeply moving Pieta by Simone dei Crocefissi. The same building also houses the **Museo d'Arte Industriale** (which, translated, would be Museum of Applied Arts) which displays furniture and decorative art from various eras and provides a window onto middle-class and noble Bolognese interiors of the 16th-18th centuries (details as above). Just off strada Maggiore, via Fondazza 37 was where the artist Giorgio Morandi lived (see p40), among the colours that inspired many of his soft abtsract paintings. At number 11 is an interior design shop in which a piece of the old via Emilia Roman road has been uncovered, complete with the grooves made by wheels.

Palazzo Ercolani
strada Maggiore 45. *Map 3, C11, p255*

This 18th-century building is a senatorial palace once inhabited by the Ercolani family who were part of the senate when the city was under papal rule. Beyond the courtyard is a classically English garden while an arcade leads to a statue-lined staircase up to rooms that are nowadays used as part of the university's Faculty of Political Science.

Casa Carducci
piazza Carducci, **T** 051-225583/347592. *Tue-Sun 0900-1300, Thu 0900-1700. Closed Mon. €2.50, concessions €1.30.*
Map 3, E12, p251

His earlier more humble lodgings being in via Broccaindosso, the poet Carducci was given this 16th-century residence as a new home by Queen Margherita of Savoy with whom he was head over heels in love. Carducci lived here from 1890 until his death in 1907 when his vast collection of books, letters and manuscripts was donated by the Queen to the citizens of Bologna in the form of the Carducci library. The building was erected on the ruins of the medieval outer city wall and since 1990 has been home also to the **Museo Civico del Risorgimento**, a museum celebrating the creation of the unifed Italian state in 1860. In celebration of the poet's love of nature, the house also has a garden, *il giardino monumentale* (monument garden), so-called after its central statue to the poet by Leonardo Bistolfi.

Via Castiglione
Map 3, B8-F9, p255

The name of this road is supposedly an elision of the words *castello* (castle) and *leone* (lion). In this instance the lion was the powerful Pepoli family (see p60) and the many buildings they owned on this road constituted their fortress.

Palazzo Pepoli and Palazzo Pepoli Campogrande
Palazzo Pepoli, via Castiglione 6-10; Palazzo Pepoli Campogrande, via Castiglione 7. *Map 4, E6, p256*

The Palazzo Pepoli, with its Guelph crenellations displaying the appriopriate aspect of a fortress, was commissioned in 1344 by Taddeo Pepoli as a sign of power to the citizens of Bologna. Opposite is an equally impressive piece of Pepoli vanity on an even greater scale, this time commissioned by a different generation, Eduardo Pepoli in the late 17th century. Less of a fortress, this was conceived as a place for receptions, banquets and festivals. Inside are many fine frescoes, some of them forcibly paying homage to the Pepolis, while the most spectacular are the 17th-century paintings by Giuseppe Maria Crespi depicting *The Allegory of the Seasons*, *The Triumph of Hercules* and *The Council of the Gods*.

Ex-Chiesa e Convento di Santa Lucia
via Castiglione 36. *Map 3, D8, p255*

Relieved of its religious functions by Napoloeon, this 17th-century church and convent was designed by Girolamo Rinaldi on the site of the 13th-century original. Set back from the porticoed road, it boasts another of Bologna's unfinished façades, with a bare and stubbly charcoal face resembling a climbing wall. It is now the *Aula Magna* (main lecturing hall) of the university, decorated with a famous Madonna by Giuseppe Mazza and inaugurated in 1988 by Pope John Paul II on the 800th anniversary of the city university.

Palazzo di Giustizia
piazza del Tribunale. *Map 3, E7, p255*

Bologna's law courts stand majestically as if in judgement them-selves looking over the flowery piazza del Tribunale. Originally a 16th-century commission as a private residence, the building has undergone numerous additions and restorations, the most notable being the harmonious façade, the central section of which has been attributed to Palladio, and the rest to Tibaldi. Restoration has also preserved the fine staircase, the courtyard and a number of fine canvasses on the first floor by Franceschini, Bigari and Giani.

Piazza Galvani
Map 4, F3, p256

Just in front of the Archiginnasio, this piazza is named after the 19th-century Bolognese scientist, Luigi Galvani, who conducted ground-breaking experiments in electricity using frogs and from whom we get the word 'galvanize'. The statue in the square shows him peering into a book with a petrified frog on the page.

Piazza Minghetti
Map 4, F5, p256

This leafy square, flanked by the imposing main post office building, is named after Marco Minghetti, one of the architects of the unifica-tion of Italy, who became the young nation's Home Secretary in its 1860 Turin Parliament. Bizarrely, he pursued a policy of local govern-ment that diced with all the regions' old local rivalries. He was res-ponsible for liberating Rome from Napoleoon III but was forced to resign when he tried to move the capital from Turin to Florence.

La famiglia Bentivoglio – patrons of the arts

The Bentivoglio family was one of the great warring dynasties of medieval Bologna. At the height of their power in 1460, Sante Bentivoglio commissioned construction of an immense family palace that stretched over most of the northern side of via Zamboni. Though not an artist himself, Sante's son Giovanni II was a keen appreciator of the arts and beauty in general and it was during his forty-six year reign that the arts flourished, in particular the school of Francesco Francia, and the city was given some of its more renowned embellishments, especially in the University quarter which was the family's stronghold (see San Giacomo Maggiore, p53). A pact between the King of France and the Pope led to his exile and overthrow and the wanton destruction of all things Bentivoglio including their palace. The family is perhaps best evoked these days in the famous jazz club that bears their name on via Mascarella and the trendy wine-bar, called Le Stanze del Tenente located in their former family chapel.

Mirasoli
Map 3, E6, p254

Literally translated as 'reflecting the sun' and so named after the reflection cast by a nearby branch of the then uncovered city canal, the group of alleys between via Miramonte and via d'Azeglio was once one of the dodgiest parts of town. A little Sicily complete with its own code of honour and culture of *omerta* – see nothing, hear nothing, say nothing – people here feared to tread lest they be knifed. It was correspondingly colourful, with many notorious osterie, most of which no longer exist, although Osteria le Mura (p152) still provides a hint of the area's disaffected past.

Chiesa di San Procolo

via Massimo d'Azeglio 52, **T** 051-331223. *0800-1100,*
1700-1900. Map 3, D6, p255

This diminutive church built on the site of an old Roman temple
has a 13th-century crypt where Proculus, the eponymous Roman
soldier was entombed, but not before becoming a saint for having
dared profess his Christian faith to his superior officer in the Imperial army. It has undergone many incarnations since then, and even
served as a warehouse in Napoleonic times, before being restored
as a place of worship in 1826. It has become famous for a piece of
early graffiti, a cryptic ancient tongue-twister inscribed on the left
façade: 'Si procul a Proculo Proculi campana fuisset, nunc procula a
Proculo Proculis ipse forret, A.D. 1393'. Roughly translated it means
'If Proculus' bell was far from Proculus, then Proculus would be far
from Proculus' Legend has it that Proculus (the Second) was a
bell-ringer who died crushed by a falling bell.

Southwest: around via del Pratello

*The southwest of the Centro Storico contrasts the elegant **via
d'Azeglio**, catwalk and hunting ground for Bologna's dedicated followers of fashion among wallet-bruising boutiques, with the boozy
uproarious osterie of the **via del Pratello** and **via San Felice**,
famous for the concentration of years-old drinking holes and the concentration of their house distillations. Amid these extremes are the
leafy squares of **piazza Galvani** and **piazza Malpighi**, the latter
providing the setting for the stronghold of the Franciscan order in
Bologna in the imposing and unusual form of the **Chiesa di San
Francesco**. The important artery of **via Saragozza** leads past the
Collegio di Spagna, symbol of Bologna's early cosmopolitan out-
look. It continues back in time, past many old bars and cafés, full of
locals and unchanged for decades, up to the **porta Saragozza**,*

gateway to the city's great colonnaded pilgrimage site on the hill, the
Santuario di San Luca.

➤➤ *See Sleeping p127, Eating and drinking p154, Bars and clubs p179*

Sights

Collegio di Spagna
via del Collegio di Spagna. *Only the courtyard can be visited.*
Map 3, C5, p254

Even in the 14th century the world's famous universities were
cosmopolitan and open to overseas students and this building,
one of Bologna's more unusual pieces of architecture for the
Hispanic references in the colour and style of its charming double
loggia courtyard, was built to house students from Spain (known
as los Bolonios). The building was a project of the Archbishop of
Toledo, briefly a papal minister of the city before being overthrown
by the council. In 1364, having paid in advance for a lavish funeral,
he bequeathed the rest of his fortune in a will that requested the
building of a college to house 24 Spanish students from noble
families. It is said that these students and their successors enjoyed
impunity from the law as they were subjects of the Spanish crown.

Piazza Malpighi
Map 3, A4, p254

Formerly a part of piazza San Francesco this is Bologna's most
colourful square, flanked down one side by a frescoed arcade that
used to form part of the church of San Francesco nearby. The
column in the centre supports a bronze statue of the Immaculate
Conception designed by Guido Reni. The Bolognese place flowers.
at the statue's feet on 8th December every year at the *Festa della
Concezione Immacolata.*

Chiesa di San Francesco

piazza San Francesco, **T** 051-221762. *Mon-Sun 0630-1200, 1500-1900. Map 3, A4, p254*

Completed between 1236-1263, this church and its convent was established as the HQ of the Franciscan order following their arrival in the city in 1211. It is a fine, even towering example of Gothic architecture with a French influence, a heavy and complex forest of spidery flying buttresses which may or may not appeal. Considering that it was badly damaged in World War II, and also used by Napoleon as a depot and customs house, it has been successfully restored. The interior, supported by octagonal trunk-like columns, conceals a number of important works of art: the beautiful marble altarpiece conceived by the Masegne brothers in Venice in 1392 depicting scenes from the life of St Francis, and the pyramidal mausoleums to *i glossari*, the university's founding lecturers and legal scholars, in the peaceful cloister of the convent next door. Set behind the altar is an unusual semi-circle of chapels notable for a tryptych completed in 1929 by the sculptress, Teresa Gruber.

Via del Pratello

Map 3, A2-4, p254

This road and the working-class area between via Sant'Isaia and via San Felice has always been renowned for its concentration of osterie and still today is a buzzing area thick with door-to-door dodgy dives and drinking joints. A Bolognese version of Barcelona's ramblas, at night it comes to life with street art, theatre and drunks.

Porta Saragozza
Map 3, C2, p254

With its three crenellated towers this is easily the most magnificent
of the 10 gates of the outer city. However, its fine state of repair is
the result of a reconstruction built in 1857 which essentially followed the design of the original but could not resist a number of
19th-century embellishments designed to herald the gateway to
the famous cloistered path to the Santuario di San Luca on the hill.

Chiesa del Corpus Domini
via Tagliapietre 19, **T** 051-331277. *1000-1400, 1600-1800.*
Map 3, D5, p254

Also dedicated to Santa Caterina, Bologna's most important female
saint, this little church and convent, restored to something like its
former glory following considerable damage in the Second World
War has a beautiful portal and also a number of frescoes by
Ludovico Carracci and friends inside.

Palazzo Albergati
via Saragozza 26-28. *Map 3, D3, p254*

Situated just before the city gate this palatial 16th-century building, distinguishable by the beautiful sandstone figures that embellish its façade, is thought at one stage to have housed Roman
public baths during the reign of Augustus. Inside is a beautiful
frieze by Lazzarino Casario.

Palazzo Bevilacqua
via Massimo d'Azeglio 31-33. *Map 3, C6, p254*

Seat of meetings of the Council of Trent in the 16th century, this
building is a good example of Renaissance Bolognese architecture,

with portals finely decorated in bas-relief and an elegant iron-balustraded balcony. Through the courtyard stands an intriguing fountain with a lion spouting water from the top of a column.

Teatro Romano
via de' Carbonesi 7. *Map 3, C6, p254*

An unusual feature for any shop, the partial remains of a Roman theatre, estimated to date back to 80BC, were discovered under what is now the Bolognese branch of the department store, Coin.

Chiesa di San Paolo Maggiore
via de' Carbonesi 18, **T** 051-331490. *0800-1100, 1700-1900. Map 3, C6, p254*

This early 17th-century church, with beautiful statuettes in the upper niches of the façade, also contains fresco masterpieces, particularly in the cupola and also *Paradise* by Ludovico Carracci and *Saint Gregory and the Souls of Purgatory* by Guercino. The façade has many swords as it was commissioned by Cardinal Bernardino Spada (*spada* means sword).

Via Barberia
Map 3, B4-C5, p254

Via Barberia is lined with many fine palazzi from the 16th and 17th centuries: **Palazzo Marescotti** at number 4 is currently the home of the Italian Communist Party, a cause close to Bologna's heart, and contains a splendid staircase with double banister designed by Giacomo Monti as well as fine paintings; at number 13, **Palazzo Salina** has decorations from the 18th century; and in the corner of piazza Malpighi, where the second circle of the old city wall used to stand, **Palazzo Rusconi** has a façade embellished by rococo ornamentations.

Northwest: around via Galliera

*Badly damaged both by Allied bombardments and subsequent bad taste in its reconstruction, the area to the northwest of piazza Maggiore is not instantly as attractive as the rest of the Centro Storico. With some notable exceptions this is an area of modern urban planning where wider boulevards replace the winding narrow alleys and concrete, glass and shiny marble replace the ageing red stone, wooden beams and porticoes. The more elegant, older central streets of **via Galliera**, **via Nazario Sauro** and **via Montegrappa** are home to beautiful, understated churches such as the exquisite **Chiesa della Madonna Colombano**, less bombastic than others in the city, as well as the important **Museo Civico Medioevale e del Rinascimento**. Much of the area's interest lies beneath the surface in the warehouses and docks of the city's ancient system of underground canals. In recent years, these forgotten industrial spaces, especially in the areas around **Porta Lame,** have been rediscovered, and either developed by the council or claimed by Bologna's experimental youth, their intriguing architecture used to transform them into spectacular hybrids of nightclub and projection spaces. The old city docks, and the tobacco factory, bakery and slaughterhouse around the **via del Porto** and **Giardino Cavaticcio** are in the process of reincarnation as exciting arts centres. At a time when urban regeneration of industrial spaces is all the rage, this area of Bologna is one of the most trendy, dynamic and surprising in the city.*

▸▸ *See Sleeping p128, Eating and drinking p158, Bars and clubs p182*

Sights

Palazzo Fava
via Manzoni 2. Map 4, B3, p256

The rooms of this old family *casa signorile* (nobleman's house) are now occupied by Bologna's prestigious Hotel Baglioni (p128).

While you may not be able to afford to stay here, a peek at the beautiful frescoes by Annibale and Agostino Carracci on the first floor can be free if done discreetly. In typical Italian style Roman ruins have recently been discovered under the breakfast room.

Museo Civico Medioevale e del Rinascimento

via Manzoni 4, **T** 051-203930. *Tue-Sat 0900-1830, Sun 1000-1830. Closed Mon. €4.13, concession €2.07. Map 4, B4, p256*

Located in the beautiful old noble 15th-century Palazzo Ghislardi Fava, with its elegant entrance courtyard, this museum inspires even those who are not immediately interested in its rich collection of artefacts from the Renaissance and Middle Ages. Here, against a wallpaper of paintings by the Carraccis and their pupils, the enthusiast can admire myriad objects ranging from pieces of armour and musical instruments to ceramics, tombs and busts of popes and dignitaries, including one of Gregory XV by Bernini.

Chiesa della Madonna di Galliera

via Manzoni 5, **T** 051-230682. *0730-1200, 1600-1830. Map 4, A3, p256*

Notable for its beautiful and delicate sandstone façade complete with figurines, this little 13th-century church, with 16th- and 17th-century additions and restorations also contains a number of important paintings in its many chapels, as well as a beautiful high altar by Francesco Bibiena.

Via Galliera

Map 2, G-E7, p253

The quiet via Galliera has always been one of Bologna's most aristocratic and well-to-do streets, lined with many fine palazzi which next door to each other illustrate very well how Bolognese architecture evolved over the centuries: 15th-century terracottas (numbers 13, 14 and 15), 16th-century proportional harmony (numbers 3-5), and Baroque majesty (number 8). **Palazzo Calzolari** at number 14 houses many frescoes behind its terracotta façade; the 18th-century **Palazzo Montanari**, now partly a public building, with its beautiful façade by Alfonso Torreggiani is also home to many frescoes; and the **Casa delle Tuate** at number 6 borrowed its corner pillar from the destroyed Bentivoglio palace.

Stazione
piazza Medaglie d'Oro. *Map 2, D7, p253*

Although not architecturally significant in itself, Bologna's station nevertheless features as a millstone on the Italian public consciousness for the devastating terrorist bomb attack that claimed 88 victims there in August 1980. The bomb was planted by neo-fascist activists targeting Bologna as a renowned outpost of leftist thinking. A plaque on the outside of the station and on the main platform commemorates the dead and close scrutiny of the station building shows a seam where it has been rebuilt.

Chiesa dei Santi Gregorio e Siro
via Montegrappa 15. *Map 4, B1, p256*

On the corner of via Montegrappa and via Nazario Sauro, this church used to be the home of the Ghisilieri family, their tower having been neatly transformed into a campanile. The side chapels inside contain famous paintings such as Annibale Carracci's *Baptism of Christ* and two frescoes by Ludovico Carracci.

Mercato delle Erbe

via Ugo Bassi 2. *Map 4, B1, p256*

Bologna's covered market has occupied the elegant neo-classical building between via Ugo Bassi and via Belvedere since 1910. Inside row upon row of stalls are laden with fresh produce from fruit and vegetables to dairy produce and meat – not the herbs you'd expect from the name. In the annex is the **Mercato del Pesce** (fish market), similarly well-stocked and more pungent.

★ Chiesa della Madonna del Colombano

via Parigi. *0830-1130, 1530-1800. Visit to the upstairs oratory by request only. Map 4, A3, p256*

One of the real hidden treasures of Bologna is the oratory on the first floor of this otherwise unspectacular 16th-century church. It is arguably the most concentrated symphony of artistic endeavour and the most beautiful individual space in the whole city. The ground floor *Virgin and Child* by Lippo di Dalmasio and other paintings by Antonio Carracci are a prelude to the stunning upstairs which seems as if it was almost a private chamber where Guido Reni, il Domenichino, Lorenzo Garbieri and other pupils of the Carracci academy could experiment with colours, forms, subjects and themes.

Teatro Arena del Sole

via dell'Indipendenza 44, **T** 051 2911910. *Mon 1530-1900, Tue-Sat 1100-1900. Map 2, G7, p253*

In contrast to Bologna's other main theatre, the Comunale, this 19th-century arena was conceived as a return to the Greco-Roman idea of a democratic theatre in the shape of a horseshoe. The theatre seats 900 people in its six tiers and was originally planned to host matinees.

Porta Galliera

Map 2, D8, p253

Reconstructed in 1661, this site marks the northern gate of the old city wall's 14th-century third circle.

The old port district, via del Porto

Map 2, E5-F6, p252

In 2000, with increased public spending triggered by Bologna's nomination as a European City of Culture, work began on developing and revitalizing the area around via del Porto which used to be the city's financial hub. This was the port area where the city's underground canals met the diverted Reno river and where the major commodities of the day, salt, marble, silk and hemp, were stored and traded. Only charitably could this area be called a true docklands in the sense of a maritime city (the river is a relative trickle), but its industrial warehouse architecture is nevertheless similar and, as is the fashion, is now ripe to be turned into a range of new cultural centres.

The old **Tobacco Factory** on via Azzo Gardino is being transformed into a theatre and film library and centre for film studies. The nearby Slaughterhouse, also on via Azzo Gardino, will be the new home and projection room of the Lumiere Cineclub. The Tobacco Factory building was once the 12th-century Benedictine monastery of Santa Maria Nova. Partially destroyed and renewed in the 16th century, it expanded to the nearby Cavaticcio gardens. In the 19th century, Napoleon closed the monastery and it was then that it took on its more secular role as a tobacco storage facility. The building was heavily bombed in World War II but still retains some of its Liberty (Italian art nouveau) features.

The old **Bakery** on the corner of via Fratelli Rosselli and via Don Minzoni, a 1917 building which played an important role in feeding the city in the First World War is being redesigned as the new home or extension of the **Galleria d'Arte Moderna** which is bursting at the seams in its space in the Fiera district (p90). The Molino Tamburi, a 18th-century paper mill alongside the Cavaticcio canal is due to open as a new university faculty of Communications as part of a design for the whole complex by architect Aldo Rossi which foresees a raised walkway crossing the Cavaticcio gardens connecting the modern art gallery to the old dock.

The **Ex-Salara**, Bologna's salt warehouse, with its sloping floor designed to let the water drain away, has already been restored after it was abandoned in 1934 and buried in rubble. Downstairs in the basement is the new home of the ultra-trendy and very cool Cassero nightclub while upstairs is also to become an exhibition centre allied to the Modern Art gallery.

Porto
Map 2, E5, p252

The redevelopment plan also forsees the restoration of the port area, recovering the quays, brick steps, cast iron bollards and original paving of its heyday. The original port was dug in the area of Pora Lame, a commission given to the architect Jacopo Barozzi, otherwise known as *il Vignola*. A hole was made for the canal and up to 50 boats could be moored in the dock at one time. Still standing is the wharf, restructured in 1928 and covered by an arch near via Don Minzoni inside which is an old 17th-century bridge. This area will become pedestrianized, and no doubt lined with cafés, together with the cleaned-up Cavaticcio gardens (currently still very overgrown), making for a scenic quasi 'left bank' atmosphere. It may be hard to believe in its current state but the good record of the local government suggests the project will be realized and a success.

Exhibition Centre and around

*The other side of the railway line begins the modern face of Bologna. In 1965 a **Zona Fiere** (Exhibition Centre) was built to cater for the increasing number of conventions, fairs and trade shows that were being hosted by the city. If Bologna has only recently become considered a tourist destination it is because until now 80% of its visitors have been businessmen. The* Quartiere Fieristico *also has a park, a theatre and the Ducati factory.*

▸▸ *See Sleeping p131, Eating and drinking p162, Bars and clubs p184*

Sights

Zona Fiere

piazza Costituzione. Info: viale della Fiera 20, **T** 051-282111, www.BolognaFiere.it   *Map 1, B12, p251*

Bologna's Exhibition Centre announces itself on the skyline with the towers designed by the Japanese architect, Kenzo Tange, in homage to the city's iconographic Due Torri. The original design for the whole area foresaw many more trees and green areas but these were never realized, leaving the complex rather bare and concrete. Aside from the halls which house the stands and exhibitions of visiting shows, the complex houses the **Palazzo degli Affari e del Commercio** (the city's Chamber of Commerce) and also the **Galleria d'Arte Moderna** (*Gallery of Modern Art, piazza della Costituzione 3, **T** 051-502859, Tue-Sun 1000-1800, closed Mon. Entry €6, concession €4.13*). This museum houses a collection of over 2000 works of modern art, both Italian and international, including some important pieces by Carlo Carra, Giorgio de Chrico, Max Ernst and Jackson Pollock.

Trade fairs

January *Arte Fiera* – Contemporary Art

February *Intimare* – Lingerie and swimwear

March *Saiedue* – Interior design; *Aipo* – fishing equipment

April Children's books and illustrators; *Futureshow* – multimedia and new technology; *Cosmoprof* – perfumes and cosmetics

May *Lineapelle* – leather goods and fashion accessories

June *Intimare* – Lingerie and swimwear (again)

September *Sana* – healthfoods

October *Cersaie* – ceramics and bathroom design

November *Lineapelle* – leather and fashion goods

December Motorshow – cars, bikes and bicycles

Parco Nord
Beyond the Fiera district.

Further along via Stalingrado (a road name which like many others in this area such as via Yuri Gagarin emphasizes the city's leftist political stance) and just beyond the ringroad, this park area is used for pop concerts, demonstrations and visiting circuses, and also has its own resident *Luna Park* where children and families can enjoy a fair experience of the real sort.

Bolognina
between via de' Carracci and via Francesco Barbieri.
Map 2, B6-A9, p252-p253

A human aspect of Bologna's modern face is represented by the small grid of multi-ethnic streets of la Bolognina (Little Bologna). These streets, full of the shops, cafés and restaurants of Bologna's immigrant communities from Africa, former Yugoslavia and the Orient add an interesting edge to Bolognese life.

Chiesa del Sacro Cuore
via Matteotti. *0800-1230 1500-1900. Map 2, C8, p253*

Further along the line of the railway the eye is greeted by the extraordinary squat lump of this modern church, built at the turn of the 20th century and with not quite the same sense of proportion as the city's other places of worship – the nave seems too tall and fat for the cupola – but awe-inspiring in a different, more aggressive way.

Teatro Testoni
via Matteotti 16. **T** 051-377790. *Map 2, B8, p253*

Opposite the church, this theatre specializes in putting on plays and shows for and involving children.

Borgo Panigale
Northwest of the old centre, beyond the ringroad.

An industrial wasteland of little note other than that it is home to the Ducati factory, where the famous motorcycles, the equivalent of a Ferrari on two wheels, are still made, and the **Museo Ducati**, (*via C Ducati 3*, **T** *051-6413111/6413259, Mon-Fri 1100-1600, Sat 0930-1330 – visit by prior arrangement only*). The museum retraces the history of the famous marque from its origins and through to the present day. Many of the original prototypes and race-winning bikes that are now being replicated as production bikes as part of the Ducati renaissance are on display.

Hills to the south

To the south of Bologna's old city walls the countryside begins to bulge above the plain in a series of lush, undulating hills which rise to the lower Apennines beyond. In the immediate vicinity are three hills, Guardia, Osservanza and San Michele, which effectively belong to the city and which are linked to it, physically in the case of the extraordinary **Portico di San Luca***, by its spiritual and patrician past. Dotted in these hills are manicured and elegant summer residences such as the* **villa Aldini** *and* **villa Spada***, beautiful monastical retreats like* **San Michele in Bosco***, places of pilgrimage such as the* **Basilica di San Luca** *and natural havens of wild meadows of the* **Parco di Villa Ghigi***. All are favourite weekend escapes with the Bolognese who come up to enjoy the peace and the spectacular panoramas over the city and the plain beyond. Apart from the unmissable walk up to the Basilica di San Luca, these places are best accessed by car. Ask at tourist information for local bus schedules.*

▸▸ *See Sleeping p131, Eating and drinking p162, Bars and clubs p184*

◉ Sights

★ Portico di San Luca
Follow the porticoes all the way from Porta Saragozza, in the southwest of the Centro Storico, up the hill to San Luca. Map 1, F6-H1, p250

Stretching for 3.6 km and encompassing 666 arches and 15 chapels en route, the construction of the portico which leads devotees and Sunday strollers up the colle della Guardia from the Saragozza gate, is the longest continuous arcade in the world. An extraordinary feat of both architectural engineering and devotion, the aim of building the portico was simply that the people of Bologna be able to reach the object of their worship, the icon of San Luca held in the Santuario di San Luca at the hill's summit,

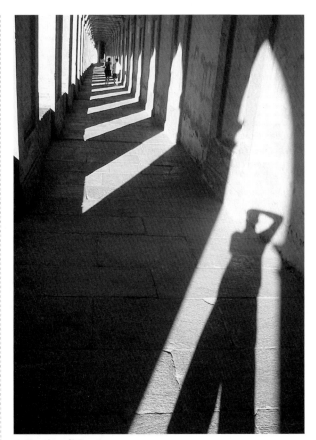

★ Portico di San Luca
Six hundred and sixty-six arches of the city's most famous portico lead from Bologna's Centro Storico up to the Santuario della Madonna di San Luca on the hill.

without getting wet or sunburnt. This flippant reason was no doubt mixed in with a sense of pride and Baroque extravagance and only conceivable by a city of considerable wealth. In a display of unity unusual among warring dynasties, each arch of the portico was financed by a combination of noble families, religious groups, merchants and artisans. Each group or family placed plaques and offerings opposite their arch in acts of worship and also to secure their own fame and immortality. Sadly most of these have now disappeared or been badly damaged, and the best example is probably the *Madonna and Child* (known as *la Madonna grassa*, the fat Madonna) by Andrea Ferri under the 170th arch. The portico was the design of the architect, Giovanni Monti. The first stone was laid in 1674 and the summit was reached in 1739. On the way up, Monti encountered several design conundrums, especially where the portico, having run along the plain, starts to lead uphill. This junction was secured by the construction of the Arco del Meloncello, an elaborate flurry of an arch designed by Carlo Francesco Dotti. At the steepest point of the incline, between the eighth and ninth chapels, a bridge was built to straddle the road.

Santuario della Madonna di San Luca

via di San Luca, **T** 051-6142339. *0700-1230 and 1430-1900. Free. For those not wishing to walk up the colonnade Cosepuri runs a minibus from villa Spada to San Luca costing €1.50 each way with departures in the morning, around lunchtime and in the evening until 1900. To reach villa Spada take bus 20 from via dell'Indipendenza.*
Map 1, H1, p250

Sitting atop the Colle della Guardia hill at a height of 291 m this grandiose basilica is the home of the icon of San Luca, the religious saint of Bologna (as opposed to Petronius, the patron saint). Records tell of a religious community on hill as far back as 1193 and an image of the Madonna has been exhibited in a small chapel there since that time. As with the best of icons, mystery and controversy surround the true origins and dating of the actual icon that rests there to this day. One legend has it that it was discovered by a Greek monk in Constantinople complete with a message that it be installed on a hill somewhere called Monte della Guardia. When visiting the Pope in Rome he was informed of the hill outside Bologna and all agreed that the icon should be sent there. In actual fact modern dating techniques show the icon to be 12th-century and one theory is that the icon is a copy made by a Bolognese painter of a 9th-10th-century Byzantine-inspired work that probably passed through Bologna during the Crusades.

The basilica had a complete overhaul in the 18th century and, with the exception of some further alterations made between 1938-1950, the current building is the design of Carlo Dotti, started in 1723 and completed by his son, Gian Giacomo in 1775. From the outside, apart from the circular dome, the design looks more fit for a villa than a basilica, with its classical columns, arches and pediments and its Palladian harmonies. Cleverly though, the inside belies the exterior shape and does resemble the form of a church. The famous icon itself is kept in the company of numerous more beautiful paintings and frescoes. Especially worth seeking out are those by Donato Creti, the *Apparition of the Virgin to Saint Dominic* by Guido Reni and the *Apparition of Christ to the Virgin* by Guercino.

Ever since 1433 when increasing religious fervour elevated the Madonna di San Luca to the status of protector of the city, the people of Bologna have celebrated their icon in what has become the city's main unique festival. Every year in May just before Ascension Day a copy of the icon is brought down the portico in procession to be installed and exhibited for one week in the cathedral of San Pietro before being returned to its home on the hill.

Villa Spada and Villa delle Rose

Villa Spada, via Casaglia 3. *Tue-Sun 0900-1300, Thu also 1500-1830.*
Villa delle Rose, via Saragozza 228, **T** 051-436818. *Map 1, G4, p250*

Beyond the Porta Saragozza are many villas, mostly former summer residences of noble families. One of the most beautiful of these is the Villa Spada, on the corner of via Casaglia. Situated by a stream in a refined Italian garden designed by Giovanni Martinietti it is a postcard of neo-classical elegance. Built at the end of the 18th century, the building was originally owned by the Marquis Giacomo Zambeccari before in 1831 becoming the headquarters of the invading Austrian army under Marshal Radetsky. It was here that the Italian patriot Ugo Bassi, after whom the city's main road is named, was tried and executed (actually at the Meloncello arch of the portico di San Luca). The villa then passed through many hands, including the Spada family, the tenor singer Antonio Poggi and, after it was damaged in the Second World War, became the property of the city. Since 1966 it has housed the **Museo delle Tappezzerie** (*T 051-6145512, Tue-Sun 0900-1300, Thu also 1500-1800, entry €2.50, concessions €1.30*), a museum which retraces the fabrics and techniques of tapestry-making across various cultures, including over 6000 examples, some of which, such as the brocatelle which covered the Christian icons in the mosque of Hagia Sophia in Constantinople, are priceless pieces of religious history. The 18th-century **Villa delle Rose** on the opposing fork of via Saragozza sits in a municipal park between an Italian garden and an English garden opened in 1930. The villa was originally built for the Cella family and is now used for occasional exhibitions as an extension of the Galleria di Arte Moderna (Gallery of Modern Art, p89). The parks and gardens of both villas are open all day.

San Girolamo della Certosa

via della Certosa. *0800-1700 in winter, 0700-1800 in summer.*
Map 1, E2-3, p250

Along via de Coubertin and via della Certosa is Bologna's main
cemetery, resting place of the painter Giorgio Morandi (1890-
1964), poet Giosue Carducci (1835-1907) and the composer,
Ottorino Respighi (1879-1936). It is not, however, just a cemetery
for the rich and famous and many more humble tombs are to be
found here such as the first two to be laid in 1801 of Giuseppe
Sarti, a baker and Maddalena Brunini, a weaver. Enclosed within
the cemetery walls is San Girolamo della Certosa, a 14th-century
Gothic church with a portico and bell tower and, inside, a strange
inverted design where a number of notable works of art can be
viewed such as the outsize paintings of *The Lord's Supper at the
Pharisee's House* and *The Baptism of Christ*, by Giovanni and
Elisabetta Sirani respectively.

Colle dell'Osservanza

*South from piazza di Porta di San Mamolo but taking the
southwesterly fork up via dell'Osservanza.* *Map 1, H6, p250*

The Colle dell'Osservanza is a hill named after the 'Observance' of
the Franciscan Reforms that began in Bologna in the church of San
Paolo in Monte. Located at the end of the road, this early 15th-
century church commands beautiful views in all directions. These
views are supposed to have been praised by Napoleon in 1805,
whose eulogy fell on the ears of his ambassador, Antonio Aldini.
Seeking to please the Emperor, Aldini went about giving flight to
the monks and in 1881 commissioned a villa, the nearby neo-classical, temple-like **Villa Aldini** (*via dell'Osservanza 35,* **T** *051-580248,
visit by arrangement only*) to be given as a present. Sadly the Emperor
never saw the completed villa as he was soon to meet his Waterloo.
The villa is closed to the public except for occasional exhibitions.

Beneath the Osservanza hill on via San Mamolo is the **Parco di Villa Ghigi** (*open daily 0900-1800*), accessible from the church of San Paolo in Monte through via di Gaibola. At 29 hectares, this is one of Bologna's largest parks, and is a beautiful rolling combination of rampant meadows and fields, and cultivated, orderly vineyards. Within its dense vegetation are a great variety of towering trees, including many oaks, beeches and a yew, and in springtime the meadows are awash with tulips and many other flowers. The park is also a natural haven for a huge variety of animals. The austere **Villa Ghigi** (*closed to the public*), is a 19th-century make-over of an old 17th-century country house belonging to the Malvezzi family. Its owner until his death in 1970 was the zoologist Alessandro Ghigi, former rector of the university and a keen environmentalist. In 1960 he donated the grounds of the villa to the city as a park on the understanding that it would be kept for the protection of Bologna's indigenous wildlife.

San Michele in Bosco

piazza San Michele in Bosco, **T** 051-6266328. *0900-1200, 1600-1800 daily.* *Map 3, H6, p244*

South from piazza di Porta San Mamolo along via Codovilla is the hill of **San Michele in Bosco**. From its summit at 132 m the **Monastero degli Olivetani** dominates the city. Built in the 14th century by Olivetan monks on the site of a Gaulish temple, the monstery has since been used variously as a fort by the Bentivoglios against the Canetoli family, a barracks under Napoloeon and now as the seat of the Rizzoli Orthopaedic institute. The interior still houses many precious works of art, among which are the carved tombstone by Jacopo della Quercia to the right of the nave, a series of frescoes by Innocenzo da Imola in the Capitular Room, and most famously, the beautiful octagonal Carracci cloister, so-called after the well-known exquisite series of 37 frescoes depicting the *Lives of Saint Benedict, Sain Cecilia and*

Saint Valerian which the famous family of painters, ably aided by Guido Reni, worked on there.

Some of the best views available of Bologna are to be enjoyed from the long esplanade that runs the length of the monastery, at 162 m, the largest covered space in Bologna.

● *From the large window overlooking the city within the monastery you can experience a strange telescopic effect whereby, if you are moving backwards, the Asinelli tower in the distance appears to grow bigger, not smaller.*

Giardini di Margherita
viale Gozzadini. *0600-midnight in summer, 0700-1800 Oct-Mar. Map 3, G/H10/11, p255*

Just beyond the southern outer city wall of the Centro Storico, between piazza di porta Santo Stefano and piazza di porta Castiglione, lie the fine Margherita gardens, inaugurated in 1879 after the wife of King Umberto I. Inspired by the Romantic design of the English parks of the 19th century, the gardens were designed by Ernesto di Sambuy from Piemonte. At the centre is a lake complete with fountains reminiscent of St James' and Regent's Park in London while majestic cedars, pines and chestnuts line the many paths and grassy areas that do their best to replicate English lawns. A number of pavilions are dotted around the park, vestiges of the Emilina Exhibition of 1888. From the edge of the main lawn you can see an Etruscan sarcophagus, part of a necropolis which was uncovered here when the gardens were created. This is Bologna's largest public park and, apart from being an excellent place to stroll, sit, think or read away from the bicycles and shadowed stone arcades, it affords lovely vistas into the rolling lower Apennines.

Museums and galleries

Biblioteca Universitaria Austere university library, home to over 900 thousand priceless tomes, p223.

Casa Carducci & Museo Civico del Risorgimento Last and favourite home of the poet Carducci and also a museum celebrating the creation of the Italian unified state in 1860, p75.

Civico Museo Bibliografico Musicale Important collection of original musical scores and manuscripts, p55.

Collezioni Comunali d'Arte Inside the citadel, various frescoes by famous Bolognese hands, p38.

Galleria d'Arte Moderna Minor abstract paintings and sculptures from the avant-garde to the present day, p89.

Museo Civico Archaeologico Locally excavated artefacts from Etruscan through to Roman times, p44.

Museo Civico Davia Bargellini Masterpieces from the 14th through to the 18th century, p74.

Museo Civico Medioevale Local Renaissance and Middle Ages artefacts in galleries decorated by the Carraccis, p85.

Museo del Patrimonio Industriale Bologna's role in industry from the 15th century and its history as a port (via della Beverara 123, T 051-6347770, *Tue-Sat 0900-1300, €4.13*).

Museo del Soldatino History and evolution of the toy soldier with thousands of models poised for battle (via Toscana 19, T 051-6236020, *Mon-Sat 0830-1230, Sun 0930-1230*, free).

Museo della Tappezzerie Fabrics and techniques of tapestry-making across various cultures, p97.

Museo di Anatomia Comparata History of the evolution of the human body, with tactile exhibits for the blind (via Selmi 3, T 051-2094243, *Mon-Fri 0830-1730, Sat and Sun 0900-1830*).

Museo di Antropologia Skulls and skeletons of Neolithic to 18th-century Italians (via Selmi 3, T 051-2094196, *open Mon-Fri 0830-1730, Sat and Sun 0900-1830*).

Bologna

Museo di Mineralogia e Petrografia Luigi Bombucci
Home to 50,000 pieces of planet Earth and elsewhere (piazza di
Porta S. Donato 1, T 051-2094926, *Mon-Sat 0900-1300*).

Museo di Paleontologia e Geologia Life on earth from
fossils and rocks to a giant dinosaur, p58.

Museo di Fisica Physics museum, arguably the home of
radio (via Irnerio 46, T 051-2091101).

Museo di San Domenico The history of the church of Saint
Dominic and the founding of the Dominican order, p73.

Museo di San Petronio Models for a bigger basilica, p.

Museo di Santo Stefano Museum piecing together the
construction and expansion of the church complex, p71.

Museo di Zoologia One of the biggest zoological collections
in Italy (via Selmi 3, T 051-2094164, *Mon-Fri 0830-1730, Sat and
Sun 0900-1830*).

Museo Ducati The history of the famous motorbike, p92.

Museo Ebraico The history and role of Jews in Bologna (via
Valdonica 1, T 051-6569003, *open Sun-Thu 1000-1800, Fri
1000-1600, €4.13, concessions €2.07*).

Museo Morandi Largest collection of works by the
20th-century painter and celebrator of small things, p39.

Museo Storico dello Studio Exploring the history of study
(largo Trombetti 2, T 051-2099020).

Museo tattile di Pittura Antica e Moderna History of art in
Braille (via Castiglione 71, T 051-332090, *bookings only, free*).

Orto Botanico ed Erbario Botanical and herb gardens, p59.

Pinacoteca Nazionale Art by the Bolgnese masters, p60.

Planetario Basic introduction to the stars and man's obsession
for reading them (via Dante 5, T 051-348946, *groups only*).

Specola e Museo di Astronomia Filled with ancient and
bizarre star-gazing contraptions, p56.

Teatro Anatomico Totally wooden dissection theatre, p44.

Apennine villages 105

The Apennines to the south have spa towns, castles and Etruscan remains.

Parma 107

Ham and cheese aside, Parma also has Romanesque architecture and great shopping.

Modena 110

Although smaller than Bologna, Modena appears more grandiose, its baroque architecture giving the true impression of a former city state.

Ferrara 112

A city of bikes and Renaissance art and planning, once hailed as the first modern city of Europe.

Imola 115

Despite Roman origins and beautiful churches, Imola is, more than anything, Formula One.

Ravenna 117

Briefly twilight capital of the Roman Empire and later lavished with Byzantine mosaics.

Rimini 117

You may simply want sea air, seafood and buzzing nightclubs, but Rimini can also offer culture.

Apennine villages

The hills behind Bologna are speckled with villages providing glimpses of rustic Italian life. They also provide the opportunity to savour the Apennine's rich flora and fauna and to take part in recreational activities, from trekking and climbing to cycling and skiing, or simply to relax at one of the area's spa towns. You will probably need your own transport to reach the deeper recesses of the region although buses do run to some of the bigger villages.

◉ Sights

Marzabotto

Museo Archaeologico Nazionale Pompeo Aria, via Porettana 13, **T** 051-932352. *0900-1200, 1500-1830, €2.50. Ruins 0800-1800. Buses at least once an hour from Bologna bus station, €10 return.*

Ten or so kilometres southwest of Bologna this village is famous for the considerable vestiges of the Etruscan town of Misa, dated to the sixth century BC and set in the beautiful wooded Monte Sole national park. Marzabotto also achieved notoriety as the place where 1800 partisan were massacred in 1944 during the last days of the Nazi occupatioin. Their names and faces are remembered on plaques on the side of the Palazzo Comunale in Bologna.

Montefiorino

Buses at least once an hour from Bologna bus station, €10 return.

Further west, atmospheric Montefiorino, with its steep approach and austere hilltop fort often surrounded in swirling mist, is another seat of partisan resistance in the summer of 1944.

Castle Route

A car is necessary to do the whole route, though buses serve individual destinations. Ask tourist information for details.

The legacy of power and paranoia among warring factions in the area is visible in the many castles that dominate hilltops. The following villages are connected by beautiful winding and tree-lined roads through the hills. Heading southwest of Bologna is **Vignola,** famous for its cherries and also the **Rocca di Vignola** castle dating back to Saint Anselm. Beyond this is the 13th-century **Castello di Serravalle** before the route reaches the beautiful castle-town of **Monteveglio**, famous not only for its imposing fortress but also the 11th-century abbey, **Abbazia di Santa Maria**, which acts as a focal point for great walks with stunning views over the countryside. At **Bazzano** the fort is a piece of typically extravagant reconstruction work commissioned by Giovanni II Bentivoglio in the 15th century on the remains of a 13th-century original. In the 18th century, the poet Ugo Foscolo was imprisoned it its tower. The castle now houses the **Museo Crespellani**, devoted to local history and archaeology. Bazzano is equally famous for its cherries and fine local wine. Further south still, **La Rocchetta Mattei** near Riola, is a castle of a different

Parmesan cheese

If you want to see how its made, free visits to one of the main dairies, the Caseificio Consorzio Produttori Latte can be arranged by Consorzio del Formaggio Parmigiano Reggiano, **T** 0521-292700. You'll meet the Master Cheesemaker, taste all sorts of different types of parmesan (and parma ham), washed down with some local wine. Be prepared for an early start. If you can't spare the time for the tour, the Caseificio, in Baganzolino, offers great truckles at cut price.

sort. Commissioned in 1850 by the eccentric homeopathic doctor Cesare Mattei, it is a fantastical fairytale hotchpotch of architectural influences from all cultures and eras resulting in a Transylavnian rhapsody of kitsch. Nearby Riola is the home of an innovative church, the **Chiesa di Santa Maria l'Assunta** , a bold and unusual 1965 Papal commission by the Finnish architect, Alvar Aalto.

Spa Towns
Salsomaggiore Terme, Azienda Autunoma di Soggiorno e Cure, viale Romagnosi 4, **T** 0524-572100/578201. *Open all year.* **Porretta Terme**, via Roma 7, **T** 0534-22062. **Castel San Pietro**, viale Terme 1113, **T** 051-234475.

There are more than 20 thermal spa resorts in Emilia-Romagna, survivors of the 19th-century fashion for relaxing in sulphurous decadence. These are the perfect places to go in order to detox and hydro-massage away the extravagances of too much rich Bolognese food. The most famous is **Salsomaggiore Terme**, 32 km west of Parma. Nowadays a bustling resort of 41 hotels dedicated to the Italian religions of health and beauty, but with magnificent Art Deco architecture, the place still retains a Belle Epoque *Death In Venice* air. For a quieter experience head to **Porretta Terme**, in prime Morandi country (you will pass through the Cezanne-like hills of Grizzana Morandi on the way), 60 km south of Bologna at an altitude of 349 m. The nearest spa experience to Bologna is at **Castel San Pietro,** only 23 km away.

Parma

The attributes of Parma read like a mouthwatering shopping list from the local delicatessen: Parma ham, Parmesan cheese and the Barilla empire that makes half the pasta in Italy. Sensuous island of affluence, elegance, sophistication, fine opera and gourmet food, the people of Parma are convinced that their city is the centre of the universe.

Retaining the snobbery which came with French rule under Napoleon's wife, Maria Luigia, they regard their town as 'la petite capitale' of Italy.

Aside from strolling and window-shopping through the sunny, yellow-tinged aristocratic streets of the Farnese dynasty that ruled here from the mid-16th to the mid-18th century, Parma has a number of imperatives on the sights shopping list.

↠ *See Sleeping p133, Eating and drinking p166*

 Sights

Duomo
piazza Duomo. *Daily 0900-1200, 1500-1900.*

Parma's cathedral is a beautifully delicate wonder of 11th-century Romaneqsue architecture with three rows of loggias and containing famous frescoes and friezes by the artists Correggio (the *Assumption* in the central cupola) and his pupil, Parmigianino, in the southern transept. The beautiful octagonal **baptistery** (hours as above), built in red Veronese marble with turrets, elaborate portals and a surrounding frieze is the masterwork of the architect, Benedetto Antelami and was completed in 1196.

Chiesa di San Giovanni Evangelista
piazza Duomo. *0600-1200 3.30-2000.*

To the east of the Duomo this church contains the famous frescoes by Correggio of the *Vision of St. John.*

Camera di San Paolo
Off via Melloni.

The back room of this former convent is famous for the daring and sensuous collection of frescoes commissioned by the abbess

Giovanna and painted in 1518 by a pupil of Correggio, Antonio Allegri.

Palazzo della Pilotta
piazza Pilotta.

Unmissable by its size, this former palace of the Farnese dynasty is now the home to a complex of museums, the most important of which is the city's art gallery, the **Pinacoteca** *(Tue-Sat 0900-1400, Sun 0900-1300, €5)*, where many spectacular works by Correggio, Parmigianino are on display, among others by the Carracci, Tiepolo, Canaletto and Leonardo da Vinci. Also within the Palazzo della Pilotta is the **Teatro Farnese**, *(entry included on gallery ticket)* entirely rebuilt in wood as it was before being bombed in 1944.

Across the river Parma stands the 16th-century **Palazzo Ducale**, former residence of Ottaviano Farnese, among an enormous and relaxing park of 18th-century gardens.

Casa Toscanini
borgo R Tanzi. *Tue and Sat 1000-1300, 1500-1800, Wed-Fri, 1000-1300. Free.*

Toscanini's birthplace: Parma was also the home of the musicians and composers, Verdi and Paganini.

Teatro Regio
via Garibaldi 16a, **T** 0521-218685/218678.

The musical tradition of the city is characterized by the opera house which attracts exacting audiences not afraid to boo during bad performances and organize *claques* (fan clubs) in support of favourites – in tune with opera's origins.

Modena

*Situated 41 km northwest along the via Emilia, Modena has always been Bologna's closest and fiercest rival. It all apparently started with a stolen wooden bucket. The Modenese were Ghibelline supporters of the Emperor Frederick II and were furious when their Guelf neighbours kidnapped his son, re Enzo. They raided Bologna and came away with the secchia rapita (stolen bucket) which thereafter became a symbol of the cities' rivalry, immortalized in a satirical poem by Alessandro Tassoni. Even today the cities mockingly squabble over supremacy in measurements of gastronomy and fast cars. The majestic **Duomo** and the impenetrable, huge bulk of the **Palazzo Ducale** dominate the city but also make it feel colder and more clinical, lacking the vibrancy and spontaneity of Emilia's capital. This is reflected in its citizens who also come across as more 'comodo' (literally 'comfortable' but meaning a cross between complacent and conceited), more snobbish and less out-going. That said, the concentric medieval centre, a tight network of labyrinthine streets built around a central square, is a pleasure to wander around and get lost in.*

▸▸ *See Sleeping p133, Eating and drinking p166, Bars and clubs p186*

 ## Sights

Duomo
corso Duomo 6, **T** 059-223474. *Mon-Sat 1030-1200, 1530-1730.*

Dominating the piazza Grande is the 12th-century cathedral to the city's patron saint San Geminiano, recognized as one of the finest examples of Romanesque architecture in Italy. The western façade is famous for its graceful columns and two majestic lions that support the central portal. This is surrounded by bas reliefs depicting scenes from *Genesis* and from the Arthurian cycle, the work of the sculptor Wiligelmo completed around 1100. The beautiful polychrome stained-glass windows inside, in particular

The Last Supper, are the work of Giovanni da Modena, completed around 1450. The cathedral's other salient feature is its 88-m high leaning bell-tower, nicknamed **La Torre Ghirlandia** (the garland tower). Half Gothic and half Romanesque, it used to contain the offending wooden bucket. The cathedral was named a UNESCO World Heritage site in 1997.

Palazzo Ducale
piazza Roma. *Closed to the public.*

Occupying the entire northeastern flank of piazza Roma, you will not be able to miss the vast 15th-century palace that was the former court of the Este dynasty who ruled Ferrara (see p113) during the Guelf and Ghibelline feuds of the 13th-16th centuries but subsequently decamped and brought affluence to Modena following defeat by Cesare Este at the hands of the Pope in 1598. This palace was the family's court and an extravagant display of fading might in its twilight years. Rather blunt and fortress-like in aspect, it is now a military academy.

Palazzo dei Musei
piazzale Sant'Agostino 337, **T** 059-222145. *Tue, Fri, Sat 0900-1900, Wed, Thu 0900-1400, Sun 0900-1300, €4.*

The Palazzo dei Musei is a complex housing the city's main museums and galleries. On the first floor is the **Biblioteca Estense**, the collected correspondence of a despotic family dynasty with its rival Emperors and Popes. It is also the home of the famous **Bibbio Borso**, the lavishly illustrated and priceless bible of Borso d'Este. On the second floor is the **Museo d'Arte Medievale e Moderne e Etnologie**, a collection of archaeological relics and artifacts of quite niche interest. The most important floor is at the top where the fabulous art collection of the Este family is hung in the **Galleria Estense**, combing paintings from the early Renaissance and masterpieces by the Carraccis, Guercino and Guido Reni, as well as sculptures by Niccolo dell'Arca. There is also a bust of Francesco d'Este by Bernini and Venetian canvasses by Tintoretto and Veronese.

Also worthy of architectural note are the clock tower of the **Palazzo Comunale** and the pretty churches of **San Francesco** (13th-century) and **San Pietro** (14th-century).

Galleria Ferrari
via Dino Ferrari 43, Galleria Ferrari **T** 0536 949714. Galleria@ Ferrari.it *Daily except Mon, from 0930-1230 and 1500-1800, €10, concessions €6. Bus 2 from Modena (every half hour).*

Visitors in search of something a little more contemporary will know that Modena was the birthplace of Enzo Ferrari, founder of the famous 'prancing horse' stable of red racing cars. He founded the factory at nearby **Maranello**, south of Modena and *tifosi* (fans) can retrace the glory years and see many classic models old and new on display at the Galleria museum.

Ferrara

Ferrara owes its Imperial aspect to the powerful Este dynasty who made the city their stronghold from the 13th to 16th centuries, elevating it from inauspicious beginnings in the middle of a fly-ridden Po delta swamp, and keeping the major artists of the day, such as Pisanello, Mantegna and Jacopo Bellini as well as poets such a Ludovico Ariosto, in work with numerous extravagant commissions. Ferrara is also the Italian capital of bikes. Locals trundle around lazily on them, lending the city an air of gentle provinciality that alleviates the domineering mortar of powers past. The centre of palace-lined arcaded streets, encircled by 9 km of ancient city wall were declared a UNESCO World Heritage sight in 1995.

❯❯ *See Sleeping p133, Eating and drinking p167*

> **The Este dynasty**
>
> The beginning of the Este family's dominance began in 1264 with Obizzo II, who with the support of Venice was summoned to reinforce the Guelf sympathizers in Ferrara. On his arrival he would have found a rather dull town. However he was to be the first of 15 Este princes to laud it over the local populace and also to bring them great wealth, art and prosperity until the fall of the dynasty under Cesare d'Este in 1598 when they moved to Modena and took much of their prosperity with them.

Sights

Castello Estense
piazza Castello, **T** 053-22992733. *Tue-Sun, 0930-1730, €5*

Dominating the main square is the brutal, prison-like castle, surrounded by a moat, the former seat of the Este family and behind whose walls lived the court, which starred, among others, the poets Ariosto and Tasso. Inevitably more elegant inside than its exterior image of power was meant to show, much of the building is now used for offices and is inaccessible. The *saletta* and *salone dei giochi* (games room), decorated by Sebastiano Filippi, contain colourful and energetic images of sports. The castle was begun at the end of the 14th century, commissioned by Nicolo II d'Este.

Duomo
piazza Trento e Trieste. *Tue-Sat 0830-1200, 1500-1830, Sun, 1000-1200, 1600-1800.*

Like that of Modena, Ferrara's cathedral is a mixture of the Gothic and Romanesque. Built between the 12th and 14th centuries, it

★ **Il Duomo, Ferrara**
Ferrara's cathedral is a grand palatial building, with lions guarding its entrance.

features work on the central portal of its façade by the same architect, Wiligelmo. Inside it is more like an opulent palace and the **museum** (**T** *053-2207449, open Tue-Sat 1000-1200, 1600-1800, free/donation*) upstairs contains a collection of important bas-reliefs and a *Madonna* by Jacopo della Quercia.

Palazzo Schifanoia
via Scandiana 23. 0900-1900 daily, €4.

Roughly translated as 'Palace for Dispelling Boredom' this palazzo was certainly built for the amusement of the Este family who had Cosimo Tura, head of the Ferrara school of painting, paint delightful escapist frescoes of the four seasons on the walls of the *salone dei mesi* (room of months), each linked with signs of the zodiac and everyday scenes of the court. Remarkably this cycle was not discovered until 1820, having been covered up by the Papacy who took control of the city in 1598. The palazzo also houses the city's main museum of local history and archaeology.

Palazzo dei Diamanti

corso Ercole d'Este 21, **T** 053-2205844. *Tue-Sat 0900-1400, Sun 0900-1300, €4.*

Further north in the grand part of the city planned by Ercole I d'Este is the 15th-century Palazzo dei Diamanti, probably named after Ercole whose nature was said to be as cold as a diamond. Diamond-shapes also feature in the nail-headed marble bossages on the façade. The palazzo houses a number of the city's museums, most notably, on the first floor, the city's main art gallery, **La Pinacoteca Nazionale** (*Tue-Sat 0900-1400, Sun 0900-1300, €3,50*) where works by Cosimo Tura and other interpreters of the Ferrara school are on display. Aside from the usual local history museums, there is also a museum to the work of the Ferrara-born film director Michangelo Antonioni, of *Blow-Up* fame.

Imola

*Imola has a Roman forum, many beautiful churches and a couple of museums, but you could be forgiven for making the only object of your visit here a trip to the world-famous **Autodromo Dino Ferrari**. Built in 1950 on the site of a Roman amphitheatre that would have witnessed many chariot races, the circuit hosts many racing events and also concerts throughout the year, but most importantly the San Marino Grand Prix.*

Imola is otherwise a nice quiet place to wander around, with an intact old centre and a grid of ancient narrow pedestrian streets opening into classic Italian piazzas complete with attendant bars, cafés and restaurants.

▸▸ *See Sleeping p134, Eating and drinking p168*

 # Sights

Autodromo Dino Ferrari

information/tickets: piazzale da Vinci 1, **T** 0542 34116. *Fri-Sun 0800-1900, www.autodromoimola.com   Taxi:* **T** *0542 28122 from the stand by the railway station or piazza Matteotti.*

For the Grand Prix the passionate *tifosi* (fans) of the home Ferrari team literally paint the town red. Situated about 30 km from Bologna, the circuit is well-signposted both from the A14 motorway and the centre of Imola.

Rocca Sforzesca

piazzale Giovanni delle Bande Nere, **T** 054-223472. *May-Sep, Sat-Sun 0900-1200, 1500-1900, entry €2.50.*

The size and power of this fortress with its four squat towers like castles from a chess set seems incongruous in the context of modern-day Imola but in medieval times it was the residence of the powerful Sforza family. It was built between the mid-13th and 15th centuries, designed by Gian Galeazzo Visconti. Its purpose now is considerably more humble as a museum of armoury and medieval ceramics, and the occasional summer concert.

Zoo Acquario

via Aspramonte, **T** 0542-24180. *Tue-Sat, 0900-1200, 1530-900, Sun 0930-1200, 1530-1900.*

Visitors looking for a day out with kids might be interested in heading for the tropical and marine fish and animals on display here.

Ravenna

Ravenna was coveted by invading forces, so much so that the Byzantines, arriving after the Goths, gave it what are generally considered to be the finest examples of their art existing anywhere in the world, still remarkably intact despite bombs and 20th-century industrial ravishment. Modern Ravenna is, however, something of a museum-city, whose treasure may only reach mosaic fiends.

◉ Sights

The mosaics are scattered in various locations around town, in the **Museo Arcivescovile** and **Battistero** on piazza Arcivescovile (*both open daily from 0900-1900, entry €1.80*) and in the **Basilica di Sant'Apollinaire Nuovo** on via di Roma. By far the most famous and richest concentration of mosaics, however, is to be found in the area around the **Basilica di San Vitale** (*via Fiandrini, T 054-434266, Jun-Oct 0900-1900*), itself a wonder of geometric Byzantine design, built in 548 and the model for the Hagia Sofia in Istanbul. Inside the basilica and across the lawn in the **Mausoleo di Galla Placidia** is a remarkable mind bogglingly untricate tapestry of mosaics.

Rimini

Nowadays the Italian equivalent of Ibiza, it is hard to believe Rimini was once an important Adriatic port. Rimini's hidden depths imclude Roman ruins and the fact that it was the birthplace and psychological inspiration of the film director Federico Fellini, whose film Amarcord *records his childhood here.*

*Rimini's **Arco d'Augusto**, dated to the year 27BC is one of the oldest surviving Roman arches in Italy. Older still is the five-arched bridge of **Ponte di Tiberio**, built in 22 BC out of white Istrian stone.*

▸▸ *See Sleeping p134, Eating and drinking p168, Bars and clubs p186*

Sights

Tempio Malatestiano

piazza San Francesco. Tue-Sat 0830-1230, 1700-1900, Sun 1600-1900. €3.60.

It was not really until the 15th century that Rimini reached the apogee of its power under the extraordinary prince-inventor-scientist-strategist-humanist, Sigismondo Malatesta. It is to him and his love for his third wife, Isotta degli Atti, that the city owes the magnificent and eclectic pagan Tempio Malatestiano. Originally a Gothic church to Saint Francis, Malatesta had its façade transformed by Alberti to reflect the motifs of the Arco d'Augusto. The pagan theme continues inside with angels, cupids, roses and elephants by Agostino di Duccio adorning the side chapels. The crucifix in the chapel of Isotta has been attributed to Giotto and the walls of the Reliquary Chapel are adorned by a magnificent and indulgent fresco of *Sigismondo praying at the Feet of Saint Sigsmondo* painted in 1451 by Piero della Francesca.

Beaches

Rimini's beaches are heavily signposted from bus and train stations.

Riccione and Cattolica are the two main beach resorts but the Italian concept of a beach is unlikely to coincide with that of visitors. As elsewhere in Italy, the whole coast has been carved up into *bagni*, private beaches the size of postage stamps which attract varying degrees of snobbery according, it would seem, to the colour of the parasols and deckchairs. There are virtually no public places to enjoy. You will be sandwiched between other towels, quickly have sand kicked in your face by a nearby game of beach tennis, or be pestered by one of a sweltering army of watch/sponge/glasses/you-name-it vendors. That said, the views of pectorally perfect men and glossy gilded lilies are fantastic.

Due to the city's prominence as a centre for business, Bologna is well-stocked with hotels, although those outside the Centro Storico have been conceived for the business traveller and are blandly decorated. During trade fairs capacity is quickly exhausted, so book well in advance. Every effort should be made to stay in the old centre, even for the sake of a few stars, since that is where you will want to be for both sights and atmosphere. Hip and contemporary design hasn't really hit Italy's hotels. Most are old and architecturally interesting buildings decorated with 1970s interiors and an assortment of dreary furniture. Rooms in central hotels are rarely spacious due to the medieval proportions. Budget options are improving with the concept of 'bed and breakfasts' breaking through (try www.bedandbreakfastbologna.com). With porticoes and narrow streets, if you are looking for a view, ask for a room high up. These are also quieter, though for absolute insulation from mopeds you will need to forgo the view for a room over a courtyard.

€ **Price**

Sleeping codes:

LL	€300 and over	C	€75-100
L	€250-300	D	€50-75
AL	€200-250	E	€35-50
A	€150-200	F	€25-35
B	€100-150	G	€25 and under

Prices are for a double room in high season

Most rooms have en-suite bathrooms although dimensions often dictate that this will have a shower rather than a bath. Few hotels have single rooms and solo travellers will usually have to pay a supplement. Payment by card is generally accepted in the bigger hotels, but others will prefer, or in some cases only, accept cash. A hotel tax of 10% is usually included in the bill, as is breakfast. However, you will have a more authentically Italian experience if you start the day with a coffee and pastry at one the city's multitude of bars.

Outside the city, Modena's narrow medieval streets offer a number of pleasing hotels for a stopover but booking ahead is essential and there are few budget options. In Rimini some might argue that sleeping is for the daytime on the beach but there are some alternatives. Imola's hotels are unspectacular and the city might be better done as a day-trip from Bologna.

Centre: piazza Maggiore and around

AL **Cappello Rosso**, via De' Fusari, **T** 051-261891, **F** 051-227179, www.alcappellorosso.it *One block west of via D'Azeglio, near piazza Maggiore.* *Map 4, E2, p 256* Over 600 years old, this hotel reputedly lodged the builders of the Basilica San Petronio as it was the only place with hot water. The 35 rooms are very comfortable, if a little dark. The attic suite on 4th floor is especially cosy. The hotel has disabled facilities and parking for a supplement.

AL Commercianti, via de' Pignattari,11, **T** 051-233052, **F** 051-224 733, hotcom@tin.it *Just south of piazza Maggiore.* *Map 4, E3, p256* Next to the basilica of San Petronio, ask for a room on 3rd floor overlooking the church, nearly within touching distance. Suite 319 is especially well-decorated. This hotel used to be part of the town hall and still retains some original woodwork in its structure. Recently restored it has a garage and modern facilities.

AL Orologio, via IV Novembre, 10, **T** 051-231253, **F** 051-260552, www.bolognahotel.it *A stone's throw from the southwest corner of piazza Maggiore.* *Map 4, D2, p256* On a pedestrian street with 32 rooms, some with fine views over the palazzo comunale, a garage and a tearoom. The eponymous clock is on the façade (it doesn't strike at night). The walls have accidentally retro fabric designs.

460

A Roma, via d'Azeglio 9 **T** 051-226322, **F** 051-239909, hotel roma@mailbox.dsnet.it *South of piazza Maggiore.* *Map 4, E3, p256* On a pedestrian street in a prime position for shopping and walking. Classical atmosphere with marble stairs, antique furniture and English breakfast. 86 quiet rooms, some with a balcony with a view and a suite with an elegant salon. Restaurant, parking with supplement and business facilities.

C Apollo, via Drapperie 5, **T** 051-237904. *Between piazza Maggiore and the two towers.* *Map 4, D4, p256* Clean and spacious in the atmospheric alleyways of the quadrilatero.

C Garisenda, via Rizzoli 9, Galleria del Leone 1, **T** 051-224369, **F** 051-221007. *On the edge of piazza di Porta Ravegnana, very near the two towers.* *Map 4, D5, p256* Clean and friendly, run by an old couple. Rooms are on the third floor of an old palazzo and so command good views of the two towers. Best to book.

D Centrale, via della Zecca, 2, **T** 051-225114, **F** 051-223899/ 051-235162. *Between via Ugo Bassi and piazza Roosevelt. Map 4, E3, p256* This centrally located and unpretentious hotel in an old noble's house offers spacious and tastefully decorated rooms on the 3rd floor, many of which have good views to the Due Torri and over the city rooftops. The reception, bar area and salon are impeccably maintained by the owner, Werther Guizzardi.

D Galileo, piazza Galileo, **T/F** 051-237452. *South of via IV Novembre. Map 4, E2, p256* Ten economical bedrooms plum in the centre.

Northeast: the university quarter

L San Donato, via Zamboni 161, **T** 051-235395, **F** 051-230547. *Northeast from piazza di Ravegna, opposite the Palazzo Malvezzi de' Medici. Map 4, C7, p256* In a plum location under the two towers and on the edge of the university quarter. Part of the Best Western group this hotel escapes feeling like a chain hotel due to its individual period furnishings and its personal service. A terrace bar overlooking rooftops is a perfect place for an evening campari and the ice-cream stand opposite the entrance is a creamy bonus.

AL Corona d'Oro, via Oberdan 12, **T** 051-236456, **F** 051-262679, www.cnc.it/bologna *Just north of via Rizzoli. Map 4, C5, p256*
The 15th-century Azzoguidi palazzo, a hotel since the early 1800s, still retains much of its antique charm despite being recently renovated. Part of it is supported on wooden porticoes, the entrance is an elegant Venetian-style belle époque veranda and some rooms have wonderful painted wood ceilings. All 35 rooms have en-suite shower facilites. There is a breakfast room but no restaurant. Bicycles, guided tours, theatre tickets, discounts at restaurants and cookery courses all available on request. Classical music concerts are sometimes organized in the mornings. Garage at extra cost.

AL Tre Vecchi, via dell'Indipendenza 47, **T** 051-231991, **F** 051-224143, trevecchi@dada.it *Just south of piazza VIII Agosto. Map 2, G7, p253* An elegant hotel with a classic tasteful turn-of-the-century décor in pale green shades. 96 airy and well-appointed rooms with all modern comforts.

B Cavour, via Goito 4, **T** 051-228111, **F** 051-222978. *Off via dell' Independenza north of the Cattedrale di San Pietro. Map 4, A4, p256* Very central and comfortable if unspectacular. Rooms with en suite bathrooms and a/c.

B Donatello, via dell'Indipendenza 65, **T** 051-248174, **F** 051-248174. *Just to the west of piazza VIII Agostso. Map 2, F7, p253* Bland but comfortable rooms on this main street. Avoid the rooms at the front which can be noisy.

C Holiday, via Bertiera 13, **T** 051-235326, **F** 051-235326, info@hotelholiday-bo.com *Off via dell' Independenza between piazza Otto Agosto and the Cattedrale di San Pietro. Map 2, G7, p253* This functional and well thought out establishment alternates opening weeks with its partner hotel, the University (see below) in July and August. Studios and kitchens are available for longer visits. Single rooms have large beds. Bicycles for hire.

C Paradise, via Cattani 7, **T** 051-231792, **F** 051-234591, www.informatutto.it/hotelparadise.net *Off via dell' Independenza between piazza Otto Agosto and the Cattedrale di San Pietro. Map 2, H8, p253* This ambitiously named hotel has 18 rooms, the top ones with good views and architectural character. All are blandly decorated. Situated among some of Bologna's fascinating side-streets, near canals and arcaded streets, Monica and Marisa will make you feel at home. Bike hire possible.

C Regina, via dell'Indipendenza 51, **T** 051-248878, **F** 051-247986. *On the southwest corner of piazza Otto Agosto. Map 2, G7, p253* Opposite the Arena del Sole theatre and next to the market, 61 rooms decorated in a classic, English style, the better ones overlooking the rear.

C San Giorgio, via Moline 17, **T** 051-248659, **F** 051-250556, info@sangiorgiohotel.it *North of the Basilica di S Martino. Map 2, G8, p253* Reliable choice with a good atmosphere.

C University, via Mentana 7, **T** 051-229713, **F** 051-229713, info@hotel-university.com *Off via delle Moline, just south of Palazzo Bentivoglio. Map 4, A6, p256* Alternating weeks of closure during July and August with Holiday hotel (see above) the Hotel University is near the municipal theatre, perfect for music lovers.

D dell'Accademia, via delle Belle Arti 8, **T** 051-232318, **F** 051-248174/263590. *On the corner with via delle Moline Castagnoli. Map 2, H9, p253* Small, simple and comfortable choice with satellite TV and disabled facilities. The eclectic decor of its foyer and 28 rooms is one of its undeliberate charms.

D Giardinetto, via Massarenti 76, **T** 051-342793, **F** 051-342816, info@hotelgiardinetto-bo.com *East of piazza di Porta San Vitale. Map 3, B12, p255* 24 comfortable and spacious rooms just outside the city walls, adjacent to the university clinic and Porta San Vitale.

D Orsola, via Palmieri 25, **T** 051-302997, **F** 051-302997, rolima.fe@libero.it *East of piazza di S Vitale. Map 1, F11, p251* Unsophisticated rooms within staggering distance of student bars.

D Perla, via San Vitale 77/2, **T** 051-224579. *Just northwest of piazza Aldrovandi. Map 3, A11, p255* Literally meaning 'pearl' this is hardly a gem. Very much like a youth hostel, with no charm and

no English, it is at least clean and cheap. Separate bathrooms.
Rooms have a safe, toilet and basin.

D Rossini, via Bibbiena 11 , **T** 051-237 716, **F** 051-268035. *Just southeast of piazza G Verdi.* *Map 3, A10, p255* A friendly choice in prime studentland.

D San Vitale, via San Vitale 94, **T** 051-225966, **F** 051-239396. *Opposite via dell' Unione.* *Map 3, B11, p255* Under porticoes but the beauty finishes there. Simple, big, quiet rooms, sunny interior garden, basic MFI furniture.

E Rimondi Monica, via Mascarella 31, **T/F** 051-245924. *Between via delle Belle Arti and via Irnerio.* *Map 2, G10, p253* Bed and breakfast – one single room with a bathroom on the third floor, three bedrooms with bathroom and kitchen on the ground floor.

Southeast: around Santo Stefano

B Hotel Touring, via Mattuiani 1, **T** 051-584305, **F** 051-334763, www.hoteltouring.it *Just off piazza dei Tribunali.* *Map 3, D7, p255* Refurbished and well-equipped while managing to retain elegance and harmonious décor with mellow colours and touches of stucco. Non-smoking rooms, garage, solarium. Large panoramic roof terrace with a view of the Bologna hills. Bicycles available.

C Blumen, via Mazzini 45, **T** 051-344672, **F** 051-345439, hotelblumen@tin.it *Near piazza di Porta Maggiore.* *Map 1, G11, p251* Located in a completely restored old building just outside the city walls, this hotel has spacious rooms with parquet floors and sparse decoration. Private parking.

C Pedrini, strada Maggiore 79, **T** 051-346912, **F** 051-341436. *Near the corner of strada Maggiore and via della Fondazza.* *Map 3, C12,* *p255* Central accommodation on the old via Emilia. Comfortable modern rooms and facilities including interior parking.

C Porta San Mamolo, via del Falcone 6/8, **T** 051-583056, **F** 051-331739, www.hotel-portasanmamolo.it *Between via Paglietta and via Miramonte Ruini. Map 3, E6, p254* A small romantic hotel in a formerly seedy district of the historic centre, refurbished with all comforts, inside garden and a/c.

E Bonzagni, via Schiassi 52, **T/F** 051-346905. *Map1, F12, p251* Bed and breakfast in a family villa. Double rooms with separate bathroom and private living room.

Southwest: around via del Pratello

C Miramonte, via Miramonte 11, **T**3395697513, MG4058@ mclink.it *Just south of via Solferino. Map3, E6, p254* Central and cheap option near the impressive law courts.

C Re Enzo, via Santa Croce 26, **T** 051-523322, **F** 051-554035. *Western edge of the Centro Storico between via del Pratello and via San Felice. Map 2, H2, p252* Small and standard but relatively charming chain hotel with American bar. Modern and comfortable rooms. Garage parking with supplement.

D Panorama, via Livraghi 1, **T** 051-221802, **F** 051-266360. *South off via Ugo Bassi. Map 4, C1, p256* Situated on the 4th floor of an elegant building, this small and welcoming family hotel offers good value for money. Rooms range from doubles to four-bed rooms but none is en-suite. The shared bathrooms down the corridor are kept very clean.

D Saragozza, via Senzanome 10, **T** 051-330258, **F** 051-733374. *North of via Saragozza between via del Fossato and via Nosadella.*

Map 3, C4, p254 A cheap and cheerful option in one of the area's most atmospheric streets, not far from the osteria of the same name.

E Senzanome, via Senzanome 14, **T/F** 051-6449245, www.users @iol.it/coruzzi/B&B *North of via Saragozza between via del Fossato and via Nosadella. Map 3, C4, p254* The hotel with no name. First floor accommodation, 10 minutes from piazza Maggiore. One double with private bathroom and turn-of-the-century furniture.

E Stefania Gomarasca, viale Pepoli 26, **T/F** 051-6447437. *On the southwest edge of the Centro Storico, just north of via Ugo Foscolo. Map 3, B1, p254* Closed Jun-Sep. Ten minutes from the centre in a 1930s building. One double en-suite with period furniture located in private wing of a private residence. Parking and garden.

Northwest: around via Galliera

LL Baglioni, via dell'Indipendenza 8, **T** 051-225 445, **F** 051-234 840, ghb.bologna@baglioni-palacehotels.it *At the southern end of via dell'Independenza. Map 4, B3, p256* On the busy main drag up to piazza Maggiore, to judge by the bill this is Bologna's only luxury address. The hotel, however, is beginning to look a little tired, especially in the 125 rooms beyond the foyer. That said, it is in a fine 16th-century building with a grand entrance under the porticoes complete with gloved and uniformed porters. There are frescoes by the Caracci brothers in the foyer and hallways, a health suite, and if you don't feel like venturing out for supper there is the renowned Caracci restaurant (with more frescoes by the masters).

A Alexander, viale Pietramellara 47, **T** 051-247118, **F** 051- 247248. *Opposite the station just off piazza delle Medaglie d'oro. Map 2, D6, p252* Modern but unspectacular 'luxury' hotel with all business facilites and mod cons. The back rooms overlook a garden.

A Excelsior, viale Pietramellara 51, **T** 051-246178, **F** 051-249448. *Opposite the station just off piazza delle Medaglie d'oro. Map 2, D7, p253* A modern, functional hotel with standard comfortable rooms near the train station. Overtly designed for business travelers although the minimalist chic foyer and bar area, a homage to Philip Stark, manages to attract an evening crowd.

A Internazionale, via dell'Indipendenza 60, **T** 051-245544, **F** 051-249544, www.monrifhotels.it *On the corner of via dei Mille. Map 2, F7, p253* Comfortable and popular with business travellers. 120 elegant and recently refurbished rooms furnished in classic luxury with marble and tiled bathrooms. Large garage.

A Jolly de la Gare, piazza XX Settembre, **T** 051-248921, **F** 051-249764. *Map 2, E7, p253* A clean and convenient modern chain hotel opposite the train station, bland and comfortable but with the odd period touch. Rooms on the top floors are decidedly more spacious than on the lower floors. The popular restaurant downstairs is open to the public and frequented by locals.

A Palace, via Montegrappa 9, **T** 051-237442, **F** 051-220689, www.hotelpalacebologna.com *Map 4, B2, p256* An independent 1930s style hotel in a 17th-century building. Stylish and gracious with mellow wood furnishings and decoration by Raphael in one of the lounges. 113 quiet and sunny rooms with private parking and some, on fifth floor, with great views over rooftops and towers. Ask for the more spacious rooms in the old part of the hotel which also have turn-of-the-century pictures and furniture. Convention room.

A Sofitel, viale Pietremellara, **T** 051-248248, **F** 051-249421. *Opposite the station just off piazza delle Medaglie d'oro. Map 2, D7, p253* A modern, well-equipped hotel, popular with businessmen due to conference facilities. The restaurant, Risbo, has a large square turn-of-the-century salon and traditional Bolognese dishes.

B Astoria, via Fratelli Rosselli 14, **T** 051-521410, **F** 051-524739, www.astoria.bo.it *Between via Don Minzoni and Giardino G Fava. Map 2, E5, p252* Comfortable modern rooms, 300 m from the station with a garden and inside garage. Bicycles for hire.

B Due Torri, via Usberti 4, **T** 051-269826, **F** 051-239944, info@hotelduetorri.it *North of via Ugo Basso near Chiesa di S Colombano. Map 4, B1, 256* 14 recently refurbished rooms 50 m from piazza Maggiore.

B San Felice, via Riva Reno 2, **T** 051-557457, **F** 051-558258, www.hotelsanfelice.it *On the corner with via San Felice. Map 2, G2, p252* Quiet and comfortable rooms with modern facilities in an unremarkable building.

C Atlantic, via Galliera 46, **T** 051-248488, **F** 051-251538, www.imieiviaggi.com/dim *West of piazza Otto Agosto. Map 2, F7, p253* A simple and economic option situated in one of Bologna's more elegant streets.

C Bentivoglio, via Marconi 18, **T** 051-6641111. *Opposite the Terminal Alitalia building. Map 2, F6, p252* Modern, efficient hotel on a busy and ugly street, but with all necessary facilities and helpful service.

C Cristallo, via San Giuseppe 5, **T** 051-248574. *West of piazza Otto Agosto, off via dell'Independenza. Map 2, F7, p253* Plain and simple rooms in a convenient location.

C Metropolitan, via dell'Orso 6, **T** 051-229393, **F** 051-224602, www.notelmetropolitan.com *Off via dell'Independenza opposite via Bertiera. Map 2, G7, p253* Refurbished modern and comfortable rooms, most with en-suite facilities.

C **Millennium**, via Boldrini 4, **T** 051-6087811, **F** 051-6087888, info@hotelmillenniumbologna.it *One block south of piazza delle Medaglie d'oro, near the station. Map 2, D7, p253* A well-appointed, superior and relatively economical take on functional modern hotels.

C **Porto**, via del Porto 6, **T** 051-247926, **F** 051-247386, www.nuovohoteldelporto.com *Southeast of piazza dei Martiri. Map 2, E5, p252* A/c rooms with satellite TV in a modern and uninteresting structure but in an interesting revitalized part of town. Mini apartments also available.

D **Marconi**, via Marconi 22, **T** 051-262832. *Opposite the Terminal Alitalia building. Map 2, F7, p253* A rare budget hotel in the old centre, noisy unless you can get a room overlooking the interior.

D **Patrizia Pozzati**, via Galliera 70, **T/F** 051-241580. *One block west of the parco della Montagnola. Map 2, E7, p253* Family lodging with three double rooms and two separate private bathrooms.

E **Accogliente Bologna**, via N Sauro 26, **T/F** 051-237498. *Three blocks north of via Ugo Bassi. Map 2, H6, p252* One double room with three beds, one single, separate bathroom, a/c, garage and terrace.

Outskirts of Bologna

B **Best Western**, via A Magenta, **T** 051-372676, **F** 051-372032, www.bestwestern.it/city-bo *Map 1, B9, p251* In a nice garden setting between the centre and the fair district, within walking distance of both. Free parking.

C **Garden Hotel**, via Emilia 29, Crespellano, **T** 051-735200. A pleasant and family-run out-of-town hotel in a converted villa. The rooms are spacious, comfortable and tastefully decorated with rustic touches, while the service is courteous and efficient. Breakfast is unusually notable with tasty homemade cakes and jams.

C Il Guercino, via L Serra 7, **T** 051-369893, **F** 051-369893, guercino@guercino.it *Map 2, B8, p253* Quiet and budget option close to train station. 30 quiet rooms overlooking an interior courtyard, nice bar and communal areas. Inside parking.

The two **youth hostels** are 6 km outside the city. *Buses 36 and 37 from the station. Curfew 2330*. **San Sisto**, via Vaidagola 14, **T** 051-519 202, is the older, while **Due Torri**, via Viadagola 5, **T** 051-501810, was purpose built for passing backpackers.

Camping Hotel – Citta di Bologna, via Romita 12/4, **T** 051-325016, **F** 051-325318, www.hotelcamping.com *Northern end of via Stalingrado*. A relative oasis in a verdant setting near the fiera district, with a swimming pool. A cross between a hotel and a campsite with more facilities than you could need for camping. Otherwise the two nearest campsites are further out towards the lower Apennines: **Piccolo Paradiso** at Sasso Marconi, **T** 051-842680, about 15 km out or, for naturists only, **Ca'lescope** in Marzabotto about 25 km away. Both are open all year round. For other possibilities check www.emiliaromagnaturismo.it In Bologna they have an office at via Aldo Moro 10, **F** 051-284122, no **T**.

Agriturismo is a government subsidized initiative aimed at supporting the rural economy by promoting lodgings in Italy's countryside. The bonus is their location for exploring the deeper countryside. **Cavaione**, the only agriturismo near Bologna, is 6 km south (*via Cavaioni 4 in Paderno, **T** 051-589006, **F** 051-589060, tcavaione@oil.it Mar-Dec*). It offers beautiful views from a rustic setting with large comfortable rooms in a 1970s villa. One single, two doubles with two shared bathrooms, €25-30 per head per night.

Breakfast is extra. You can also rent apartments by the week (€25 per person per day). Guided tours and horseriding are also offered.

Parma

A Hotel Torre, via Ghirardi 8, San Michele Torre, Felino, **T** 0521-831491. A romantic 16th-century castle-like setting. Small and intimate with12 rooms in a wonderful setting. Good restaurant. Outside town but well worth the journey.

B Hotel Verdi, viale Pasini 18, **T** 0521-293539. Opposite the parco Ducale, this elegant Liberty-syle hotel has refined, marble interiors.

C Croce di Malta, borgo Palmia 8, **T** 0521-235643. Central and predictable, but comfortable. Also has a decent restaurant.

Modena

A Canalgrande, corso Calagrande 6, **T** 059-217160. Located in a 17th-century, neoclassical palazzo with marble column and frescoes, this hotel has all mod cons and comfortable rooms.

C Liberta, via Blasia 10, **T** 059-222365. A newly refurbished and efficient hotel plum in the centre.

C Principe, corso V Emanuele II, 94, **T** 059-218670. Well-appointed rooms in an elegant palazzo in the old centre.

Ferrara

A San Paolo, via Baluardi 13, **T** 0532-762040. Comfortable and clean accommodation in a nice location by the river.

D Casa degli Artisti, via Vittoria 66, **T** 0532-761038. Simple but charming rooms in the medieval quarter.

Imola

C Molino Rosso, via Statale Selice 49, **T** 054-640300. A family-run and friendly if unspectacular hotel with a decent restaurant.

Rimini

LL Rimini , parco F Fellini 1, **T** 0541-56000. The prestigious sea-side address. Luxurious rooms, sports facilities, cool restaurant.

A Esedra, viale Caio Duilio, **T** 0541-23421. Journey back in time to turn-of-the-century spa days. Gracious salons, a garden and pool.

D Biancamano, via Cappellini 1, **T** 0541-55491. All mod cons for maximum comfort, with ample parking, gardens and a pool.

Eating and drinking

Bologna is to food what Milan is to fashion and the city strains with restaurants in the same way your belt might after you have spent a few days helplessly gorging yourself on their typically abundant and delicious food. Although famous internationally for its cuisine, Italy is a land full of deeply felt regional identities where local food specialities are the expression of a region's identity. It is not unusual to hear Italians from different areas claiming theirs to be the home of the best food in Italy. Rich, substantial and varied, *la cucina bolognese* has a better claim than most, something which the *bolognesi* will lose no opportunity to remind you of. But whatever your view, suffice it to say that food here is taken (and eaten) seriously and copiously; in a city with street names such as vicolo Baciadame (Lady-kisser Lane) and via Fregatette (Tit-rubbing Street) food is enjoyed with gastro-erotic pleasure. And as the city's nickname *la grassa* (the fat) suggests, you are unlikely to go home anything other than totally sated, and certainly no thinner.

Eating places range from the formal *ristorante,* to the more homely and rustic *trattoria,* to the famous lively pub-like *osteria,* although several have adopted such prefixes in search of *ye olde* authenticity and there are many hybrids that blur these distinctions. The majority of places, instead of cutting-edge design, share variations on the same typical décor of wooden beams and vaulted ceilings and the old values of home-made hand-made dishes prepared with fresh, local, seasonal produce according to recipes handed down over generations. Don't be surprised if you are not presented with a menu. Chefs will usually take pride from insouciantly reeling off the huge range of dishes on offer and, provided the ingredients are in season, will often be able (and proud) to rustle up anything (Italian) you may ask for with characteristic *disinvoltura.*

Despite the abundance of restaurants it is advisable to book ahead. Watch out for days when restaurants are closed and, if visiting in August, be prepared for many restaurants to be closed for holidays. Lunch is usually served between 1200 and 1500 and most places will not open in the evening before 2000 with their kitchens closing at around 2300. In Rimini Spanish hours are fashionable at the height of summer and restaurants tend to fill up around 2330. Late-night munchies can be satisfied in many osterias. It is worth noting that there are fantastic restaurant options outside the Centro Storico and in the surrounding hills. These are accessible by taxi and provide a change from the porticoes and vaults, sometimes with spectacular vistas.

Open to influence and invention, Bologna is better stocked than many Italian cities with ethnic restaurants (Indian, Chinese, Greek and Middle Eastern), which can make a refreshing change from the feasts of regional fare.

€ **Eating codes**

€€€ €30 and over

€€ €20-30

€ €20 and under

Price per head for a two-course meal excluding wine

Centre: piazza Maggiore and around

Restaurants

€€€ **Nuovo Notai,** via de Pignattari 1, **T** 051-228694. *Closed Sun. Map 4, E3, p256* A must for all lovers of mushrooms and truffles which form the base for the stuffings, sauces and aromas of many of the creative Umbrian-Tuscan dishes. The green asparagus tart is also delicious, as is the pudding, *castagne alla fiamma* (flaming cheshuts). This is an elegant if slightly pricier restaurant than most in a very central location.

€€€ **Pappagallo**, piazza Mercanzia 3, **T** 051-231200. *Closed Sun. Map 5, D9, p256* One of the city's most famous restaurants. In the heart of medieval Bologna set in the walls of an old 14th-century palazzo right underneath the two towers, this historic and elegant restaurant, in a single high-ceilinged, echoing hall, has an accordingly formal and refined atmosphere (although this is rather detracted from by the sycophantic display of self-reverential photographs at eye level). The menu offers a variety of Mediterranean dishes as well as the Bolognese classics and a fine selection of local wines and after-dinner liqeurs.

€€€ Rodrigo, via della Zecca 2, **T** 051-220445. *Closed Sun.* *Map 4, C1, 256* Located in the building that was formerly the National Mint, Rodrigo has been a restaurant for 50 years, serving international and local dishes in a refined environment of wall-to-wall wine bottles (the wine list is accordingly varied and extensive) and chandeliers. Popular for after-show and late-night diners, it is particularly renowned for its white truffles, porcini and agaric mushrooms between September and December.

€€€ Torre de' Galluzzi 5, corte Galluzzi 5 **T** 051-267638. *Closed Sun, at time of writing closed for refurbishment.* *Map 4, F3, p256* Located in one of Bologna's medieval towers this restaurant offers Southern cuisine from Puglia, the heel of Italy, and therefore has a bent towards fish and seafood, as well as the signature orecchiette (pasta in the shape of little ears).

€€ Da Gianni – A la Vecia Bulagna, via Clavature 18, **T** 051-229434. *Closed Mon and also Sun evenings in summer.* *Map 4, E5, p256* Small and rustic, this is another of Bologna's institutions that has remained unchanged since the 1950s. Fresh hand-made pasta, excellent *bollito misto*, polpettone and *fritto misto*, to be washed down with a fine locally produced San Giovese or Albana. When in season try the chestnut tortelloni.

Trattorie

€ Bistrot Tamburini, via Caprarie 1, **T** 051-234726, www.tamburini.com *Closed Tue, Thu pm and Sun. Sat pm in summer.* *Map 4, D5, p256* Set in the back of this the most mouth-watering of Bologna's fresh food shops is a simple self-service canteen where daily until 1700 you can sample on site your own tailor-made selection of the hanging garden of delicacies spread out around the shop and wash them down with a picher of draught wine. It is usually packed at lunchtime so if you can bear to wait a little you will be able to eat in peace. Deliveries can be arranged to any address within Italy. Parties can also be organized here.

Cafés

Torinese, piazza re Enzo 1a, **T** 051-236743. *Map 4, D4, p256*
Arguably home of the best hot chocolate in town.

Rosa Rose, piazza Re Enzo. *Map 4, D4, p256* The sister café to the trendy bar-restaurant in via Clavature this is a chic new bar with animal print sofas and designer lamps.

Roxy Bar, via Rizzoli 9, **T** 051-233746. *Map 4, D5, p256*
Immortalized in a song by the famous local-born Italian rocker, Vasco Rossi, this bar is a place of pilgrimage for his fans as the graffiti in the shrine-like toilets testifies. Under the arcades beneath the two towers, this is a small and unremarkable but good place to start the day. In the evening, in tune with the song's lyrics, it is known for its selection of whisky, port and sherry. Translated as 'A Life on the Edge', *Una Vita Spericolata* by Bologna-born rocker, Vasco Rossi became the angst anthem for Italian youth in the late 1980s. In it the singer tells of his desire to shake free from the claustrophobic conservatism of modern Italy, dare a little and have the life of a film character, specifically 'a life like Steve McQueen'. The chorus then dreams of how he would meet up in the Roxy Bar in Bologna with his friends, all similarly would-be McQueens, and exchange tales of their exploits.

! The cappuccino is named after the Capucin monks. They didn't invent it – the coffee is named after their habit of brown cloaks with white hoods.

Northeast: the university quarter

Restaurants

€€€ Ghiotto, via San Vitale, 9/B, **T** 051-26 68 51. *Closed Sun except holidays. Open late.* *Map 4, D6, p256* Traditional Bolognese restaurant set in a cellar-like stone cavern complete with fireplace. The rustic atmosphere is rendered more formal by the service and Renaissance details in the decor. Offers regional and broader Italian and even Spanish dishes owing to the Sicilian origins of chef and owner.

€€€ Franco Rossi, via Goito 3, **T** 051-238818. *Closed Sun except during trade fairs.* *Map 4, A4, p256* More of an exclusive drawing room this small and welcoming restaurant is a delight, both for its quiet and intimate atmosphere and for its slightly lighter and more modern take on heavy Bolognese traditions. Franco will serve and advise you while his brother Lino works magic behind the scenes.

€€ Benso, vicolo San Giobbe 3, **T** 051-223904. *Closed Sun.* *Map 4, C5, p256* Tucked down an intriguing little passage on the edge of the old Jewish ghetto this is a fun restaurant. A series of interlinked sexily-lit little rooms are always full and popular with footballers and fans of Bologna FC (as you can tell by the decor and strange murals) especially the day after a match. It is a famous restaurant founded in 1903 and now owned by Beppe and Piero who stick to Bolognese traditional cuisine for the main courses while their southern roots come through in unmissable desserts like *gelato ripieno all frutta* and *cassata siciliana*. There is an interior garden for eating outside in summer.

€€ Bentivoglio, via Mascarella, 4/B, **T** 051-265416, www.affari. com/bentivoglio *2000-0200. Closed Mon.* *Map 4, C5, p256* Set in a basement evocative of the cellars of the Bentivoglio palace this is the best place to hear live jazz. The Ronnie Scott's of Bologna and something of an institution in the city, the slightly disappointing food (relatively speaking, of course – this is Bologna) is compensated for by the quality of the music, the appropriately cool ambience and an extensive wine list of over 400 labels. Advisable to book, especially at weekends and if you want to eat late. See website for information on visiting artists and full programme. Short cookery courses sometimes offered.

€€ **Doge**, via Caldarese 5, **T** 051-227980. *Closed Mon*. *Map 4, D7, p256* Slightly kitsch but air-conditioned setting with tasty pizzas and Mediterranean food and fresh fish every day.

€€ **Donatello**, via Righi 8, **T** 051-235438. *Closed Sat*. *Map 2, G8, p253* An elegant restaurant with high frescoed ceilings and traditional furnishings that has been open since 1903. The menu offers a vast choice of dishes with the local specialities of boiled meat being particular tasty among the *secondi*. Try the slices of beef in balsamic vinegar. The walls tell of 100 years of popularity among famous artists and musicians, from Puccini to Bocelli. The restaurant is still often frequented by sports and showbiz personalities.

€€ **Pino**, via Goito 2, **T** 051-227291. *Closed Mon*. *Map 4, A4, p256* Wood oven-cooked pizzas and fresh Bolognese cuisine with hand-made pasta. Outside veranda during the summer.

Trattorie

€€ **Annamaria**, via delle Belle Arti 17, **T** 051-266894. *Closed Mon*. *Map 4, A8, p256* Set just behind the Teatro Comunale in the lively university district, this famous and hospitable restaurant is often frequented by actors and 'VIP' from Italian showbiz, a fact to which the photographs emblazoned all over the walls play testament.

The menu is rooted in Bolognese tradition with fresh handmade pastas and sauces centre stage. The *sfogline* can be seen kneading their stuff by day. The speciality is *tortellini alla gorgonzola*. Alernatively try the roast rabbit followed by Bolognese trifle or the crème brûlée.

€ **Il Portico**, via A Righi 11, **T** 051-221185. *Closed Wed. Map 2, G8, p253* A good value and functional restaurant with a warm decor, nice turn-of-the-century furniture set within a classic arcade. The pizzas are particularly good and the restaurant also offers a more substantial and typical menu.

€ **La Farfalla**, via Bertiera 12, **T** 051-225656. *Closed Sat eve and Sun. Map 2, G8, p253* A genuine and humble trattoria still with its rather kitsch post-war decor. Very welcoming, delicious and superb value. Another taste of the real Bologna.

€ **Le Maschere**, via Zappoli, 5, **T** 051-261 035. *Closed Sun. Map 2, G8, p253* Ingenious and spicy fish recipes combining Romagna with Egypt. Popular and small so book ahead. Specialities lobster, seafood spaghetti or risotto, *coquilles San Jacques*, and squid kebabs.

€ **Serghei**, via Piella 12, **T** 051-233533. *Closed Sat eve and Sun. Map 2, H8, p253* Originally started as a salon for card players who wanted a bit of a snack this small and honest trattoria has lost nothing of its origins. It serves wholesome, simple and abundant Bolognese dishes, perfect for famished students. Now run by the second generation family, Serghei was the nickname a group of regular visiting Russian dancers gave their father in the 60s.

€ **Toni**, via Augusto Righi 1, **T** 051-232852. *Closed Mon and Tue. Map 2, G7, p253* Easy-going pub-bar nicely stuck in the past and serving robust Bolognese classics at decent prices.

★ Le sfogline

*By day in Bologna you can still see pasta being made by hand, ready
for consumption in the evening. Meaning 'thin strips', pasta makers
are called* le sfogline *after the shape of the pastas such as tagliatelle
and lasagne that are indigenous to the city. There is a particularly
good opportunity to view the pasta makers in action, outside
Ristorante Anna Maria on via delle Belle Arti.*

Osterie

€ **Dell'Orsa**, via Mentana 1, **T** 051-231576. Open daily. *Map 4,
A6, p256* Popular student lunch hangout serving simple menu of
regional dishes all day until 0100. Great crostini, broad range of
beers. Good lively stop for lunch if you want a taste of young
Bologna. Occasional live jazz and other music.

€ **Du Madon,** via San Vitale 73, **T** 051-226221. *Closed Sun. Map 3,
A11, p255* Unprepossessing from the outside this is a typical
osteria with vaulted brick ceilings and dark wood furnishings offering typically robust and high-quality local dishes.

Thai

€ **Buddah**, vicolo de' Facchini 4, **T** 051-221920. *Closed Wed. Map 4, A7, p256* Genuine Thai cuisine with a good reputation.

Greek

€€ **Taverna Partenone**, piazza San Martino 4, **T** 051-230185. *Closed Mon. Map 4, A6, p256* An informal piece of Greece in a peaceful piazza, serving Bolognese and superior Greek cuisine. Good octopus and fish salads.

€€ **To'steki**, largo Respighi 4, **T** 051-268012. *Closed Sun. Map 4, A6, p256 Next to Teatro Comunale.* Good for whole meals or snacks – particularly at lunch – this restaurant offers more unusual Greek dishes than the typical fare and a broad range of potent wines.

Indian

€€ **Moghul**, via dell'Inferno 16, **T** 051-232911. *Closed Sun. Map 4, B6, p256* A welcoming and atmospheric place, worth a visit for a change of palate.

Middle Eastern

€ **Al Salaam**, via Centotrecento 24, **T** 051-244173. *Closed Sun. Map 2, G10, p253* A taste of the Middle East under the arcades with falafel, fatayer and mint tea. Jamil, a doctor who originally came to Bologna to get a pharmacy PhD, displays typical Middle Eastern courtesy and offers tailor-made preparations, ringing a bell to say when your dish is ready, the number of rings being the number of your table.

Latin

€€ Cubano Cohiba, via Borgo S Pietro 54/a-b, **T** 051-6390527. *Map 2, F9, p253*   Cuban cuisine with shows and live music in a lively setting.

€€ Piedra del Sol, via Goito 20, **T** 051-236151/051-227229. *Closed Tue. Map 4, A5, p256*   An air of the tropics in downtown Bologna. A lively place offering superior Mexican cuisine, shows and music. Packed at weekends so be prepared to queue and try one their excellent margaritas while you wait.

Cafés

Bravo, via Mascarella 1. *Map 4, A8, p256*   A must for the Sunday brunch served from 1200-1600 where for a reasonable flat price you can eat as much as want from a delicious smorgasbord of cold Bolognese dishes, soups and cakes in hip contemporary surroundings with Bologna's affluent youth. In a bizarre statement of retro irony in this coffee-proud country Nescafé is the height of fashion here, served up by waitresses looking like Malboro girls. An Italian take on the greasy spoon and a great place to eat off a hangover.

Del Museo, via Zamboni 58, **T** 051-246620. *Early closing Sat. Closed Aug. Happy 'hour' Thu, 1830-2230. Map 2, H11, p253*   Welcoming and retro, dark wood, sofas, alcoves and mirrors, great for tête-à-tête and romantic drinks served by Felix the funny barman. Popular with students and professors who should be studying or lecturing.

Del Teatro, via Zamboni 26, **T** 051-222623. *Map 4, B8, p256*   Opposite Teatro Comunale and supposed place of invention of the *festa della laurea* (graduation party). Pleasant and decadent atmosphere.

Del Rosso, via A Righi 30, **T** 051-236730. *Closed Mon. Map 2, G8, p253* Open since 1850 this place has a sombre and slightly empty atmosphere but the old building retains many of its original features. Local specialities and very good *crescentine* and *tigelle*.

Golem caffe d'Arte, piazza San martino 3/b, **T** 051-262620. *Closed Mon. Map 4, A6, p256* In the heart of the old Jewish quarter this is a classy all-in-one joint popular with artists and intellectuals. The walls exhibit art and there are bookshelves, newspapers and boardgames. The bar also hosts live music, film projections, and small theatre productions, while also producing fine cocktails and a decent menu. Effete, expensive but ultimately cool.

Terzi, via Oberdan, 10, **T** 051-236470. *Map 4, C5, p256* Recently opened, this sophisticated café aims to recreate the experience of the coffee salons of Paris and Venice, but offers an untypical selection of coffees and teas. The cappuccinos come served with mouthwatering fresh gratings of dark chocolate. There is also a recherché selection of fine wines and, slightly more pretentiously, different waters, all of which can be consumed either at the bar or in the small but stylish salon at the back. A great place for a luxurious breakfast if you're staying at the Hotel Corona d'Oro.

Whoopie, via Oberdan 24, **T** 051-271618. *Map 4, A5, p256* Popular café in this pedestrian street with outside tables. For a drink, snack or aperitif.

Southeast: Santo Stefano and around

Restaurants

€€€ **Antica Osteria Romagnola**, via Rialto 13, **T** 051-263699. *Closed all day Mon and Tue at midday. Map 3, D9, p255*

Comfortingly anonymous from the outside Antonio's restaurant is rustic, welcoming and always noisy, with dark wood panels, musical instruments and mirrors on the walls, and a characteristic inner courtyard. Superb local and regional cuisine tailor-made to your taste. Particularly tasty mortadella *a cubetti* and lasagne. Occasionally the meal is accompanied by a pianist.

€€€ **Drogheria della Rosa**, via Cartoleria 10, **T** 051-266 864/ 051-222 529. *Closed Sun*. *Map 3, D9, p255* This cosy restaurant run by the ebullient Emanuele Addone used to be a food store (hence its name) and still retains the original furnishings, doors and window frames. Superior dishes from all over Emilia-Romagna are served in an intimate atmosphere with an exceptional choice of wines. The mozzarella alone is beautifully juicy and sweet.

€€€ **L'Anatra e l'Arancia**, via Rolandino 1, **T** 051-225505. *Closed Sun*. *Map 3, C7, p254* Literally 'the duck and the orange' this atmospheric and young-spirited restaurant is more Romagna than Emilia, mostly based on seafood with the odd innovative fusion such as pate de foie gras with shellfish. All dishes come served with *piadina*, the traditional Romagna bread.

€€ **Buca San Petronio**, via dei Musei 4, **T** 051-224589. *Closed Thu except holidays*. *Map 4, E5, p256* Below street level, this sumptuous drawing-room style restaurant is popular with tourists but that should not deter you. The *fritto misto* is delicate and delicious, as is the mouthwatering lemon mousse to follow.

€€ **Cesarina**, via Santo Stefano 19, **T** 051-232037. *Closed all Mon and Tue lunch*. *Map 4, F7, p256* Set in the arcades overlooking arguably the most tranquil and picturesque square in Bologna, Cesarina offers specialities from all over Emilia-Romagna and particularly good fish dishes such as *Maltagliati* with moscardini fish, and has an impressive selection of international wines and spirits

Specialities

Broadly speaking the region's cuisine can be divided in two. Emilia, the western part known for its cured meats and cheeses and Romagua in the east for its variety of elaborate fish dishes.

By way of an *antipasto* (starter) there are almost as many kinds of *salami* and *prosciutto* as there are towns. The world-famous *prosciutto* of Parma should not obscure other variants on the cold meat theme such as: *culatello* also from Parma, *mortadella* ham from Bologna, the *zampone* (stuffed pig's trotter) of Modena and the *pancetta* and *coppa* (both types of ham) of Piacenza.

On the side, to help you assuage your hunger before the food arrives, you will probably be offered *cresentine*, delicious, popadum-like discs, usually for dolloping mozzarella and mortadella on.

For the *primo piatto* Bologna is also the home of stuffed pastas such as *tortellini*, *cappellacci*, and *anolini* as well as the old favourites, *tagliatelle* and *lasagne*.

And on top of your pasta who could now do without the cheese of Parma, *parmigiano*. Essential not only to sprinkle but also, when added to milk, to make the many sauces and baked pasta dishes *alla parmigiana* which define the region's cooking. Parmesan is not the only cheese though, and visitors should try the equally feety *grana padano* and also the beautifully soft cow's milk *squacquerone*.

On your side salad you might like to try a little *aceto balsamico* (balsamic vinegar) from Modena and to wash it all down a glass of Lambrusco, Albana or Sangiovese.

Hearty eaters might be tempted to find room for a delectable dessert, from the almondy and crunchy *torta sbrisolona*, or spiced *spongata* (spongecake) to the *torta di riso* (ricecake), or the perversely named *zuppa inglese* (English soup), which we simply call trifle.

to match. The speciality of the house is cannellone stuffed with thin tagliatelle, porcini mushrooms and parmesan.

€€ **Silverio**, via Mirasole 19, **T** 051-585857. *Closed Sun. Map 3, E6, p254* Hidden away in this inviting tiny side-street of old Bologna and with an entrance that seems like going into a private residence this is a delightful little restaurant with a small ante-room and a longer backroom. Classic local cuisine is combined with avant-garde dishes that stir the taste buds with new experiences. The desserts are expertly made and delicate. In pure Italian style there is a room for dedicated smokers.

€€ **Da Fabio**, via del Cestello 2, no phone. *Eves only. Closed Sun. Map 3, E9, p255* Wonderful and plentiful regional dishes in this cosy, intimate and unpreposessing little restaurant with personal service.

€€ **Bistro Hostaria**, via Cartoleria 15, **T** 051-272900. *Map 3, D9, p255* Opposite the Teatro Duse this new option set in a quiet, romantic porticoed street is a favourite with thespians. Traditional, regional dishes are the speciality.

€ **Grassilli**, via del Luzzo 3, **T** 051-222961. *Closed Wed. Map 4, D6, p256* Tucked away in an obscure part of the city this is a rare 'fusion food' restaurant in Bologna where the transalpine ideas of French chef Jacques Durussel meet Emilian traditions to surprising effect, and with a respect rare in these parts for the calorific concerns of the day. Traditionally attracts musicians and composers. With excellent service, this is one for special occasions. Book ahead.

! Bolognese legend says that tortellini are the creation of a Roman inn-keeper who, overawed by the beauty of Venus' navel, was inspired to create a pasta in its image.

Trattorie and others

€€ **Al 15 (Quindici)**, via Mirasole 15, **T** 051-331806. *Closed Sun. Map 3, E6, p254* Currently popular with a young and lively clientele. Abundant portions of Bolognese cuisine. Try the *crescentini* and the *tortelloni ai carciofi* (artichokes). Simple decor, newspapers on ceilings and refreshingly informal and insouciant service. Try and eat in the back room. Best to book.

€€ **Da Ercole**, piazza Minghetti 2, **T** 051-228848. *Closed Mon. Map 4, F5, p256* Situated on a leafy piazza here you will find typical Bolognese cuisine, good fish dishes and large salads. Perfect for a lunch stop and popular with older locals with seating outside in the summer. Ercole (Hercule if you're Belgian) also runs a few bed and breakfast rooms upstairs (www.bedandbreakfastinbologna.it)

€€ **Leonida**, vicolo Alemagna 2, **T** 051-239742. *Closed Sun. Map 4, E6, p256* Warm and mellow arts and crafts wooden interior. Sumptuous meat dishes with vegetable accompaniments and sauces according to the season. Particularly good asparagus lasagne, peas with tagliatelle and other delicious pasta dishes with artichokes and aubergines when in season.

€€ **Trebbi**, via Solferino 40, **T** 051-583713. *Closed Sat lunch. Map 3, D6, p254* One of Bologna's historic trattorias, open for over 50 years and serving simple local fare that seems to go down well with late-night stragglers and their drink.

€ **Bottega Albertini**, via dei Coltelli, 9/2, **T** 051-228 532. *Closed Sun. Map 3, E10, p255* Formerly the Sale e Pepe restaurant, this establishment serves creative cuisine, specializing in non-traditional dishes such as cream puff with hot chocolate in a romantic candle-lit setting. The fixed price of €15 per head for a meal including wine makes this one of the best deals in town.

Osterie

€€ **Degli Angeli**, via Farini 31, **T** 051-268032 . *Closed Sat lunch and all Sun. Map 3, C9, p255* In this little 'tavern of the angels' you can eat like the gods even if the pleasure of the food seems sinful – in particular the lamb cutlets . All will be forgiven.

€€€ **Dei Poeti**, via dei Poeti 1, **T** 051-236166. *Closed Mon. Map 3, C8, p255* Another of Bologna's oldest osterias located in the 14th-century Palazzo Senatorio. It owes its modern name to the custom of the Bolognese poets Carducci and Pascoli and could perhaps be accused of resting on their laurels. There are two rooms: one smaller with a fireplace and the larger where three times a week there is live music. Besides the excellent choice of Italian wines you can feast on typically wholesome Bolognese fare.

€€ **Le Mura**, via Falcone, 13, **T** 051-331772. *Closed Mon. Map 3, E6, p254* Although only 15 minutes walk from the centre, its location just inside the perimeter mean this simple, lively and informal restaurant, where typical Bolognese fare is served in generous portions and without ceremony, is largely ignored by tourists. Great for entertaining large groups. Book in advance.

€€ **L'Infedele**, via Gerusalemme 5, **T** 051-239456. *Closed Mon. Map 4, E7, p256* Small bohemian joint with classic snacks and some *primi piatti* for those with more of a twist.

Vegetarian

€ **Clorofilla**, strada Maggiore 64, **T** 051-235343. *Closed Sun. Map 3, C11, p255* One of Bologna's few lifestyle-eating propositions with a minimalist-naturalist décor this restaurant offers healthy dishes mixing ingredients from all round the world complete with explanations of their healthy properties. Particularly big on salads which might provide light relief for non-vegetarians. There is a wide selections of teas and tisanes, and even the beer and wine are organic.

Cafés and gelaterie

Bricco d'Oro, via Farini 6, **T** 051-236231. *Map 3, C7, p255* Very good hot chocolate topped with mountainous cream. Also a broad selection of bites at aperitif time.

Dei Commercianti, strada Maggiore 23/c, **T** 051-266539. *Mon-Sat until 2200 Map 4, D7, p256* Extra special and varied coffees, from *liscio* (straight) to *turchetta* (with with a shot of liqueur) to *sbagliato* (literally "wrong") – with a drop of chocolate – as was in vogue in the 18th century. Popular with up-and-coming arty types, British Council teachers, writer Umberto Eco and ex-prime minister Prodi. Great spot for *frizzantini* and tiny crustless sandwiches. Also popular at aperitif time for its wines and cocktails.

Morandi, piazzetta Morandi 1, **T** 051-342734. *Map 3, D12, p255* An anonymous bar that serves perhaps the best cappuccino in town: thick and creamy and full of flavour due to a slightly more patient preparation than elsewhere.

Zanarini, piazza Galvani 1, **T** 051-261891. *Map 3, C7, p255* At the time of writing closed for refurbishment but long famous for its long drinks, pastries, cakes and great coffee, Zanarini had perhaps fallen from grace locally in recent years or was at least yesterday's Café de Paris, frequented by a more staid clientele. It is still well worth a visit for its elegant salon with period furnishings and sofas, or a post-passeggiata aperitif.

Gelaterias

Sorbetteria Castiglioni, via Castiglioni 44, **T** 051-233257.
1730-2345. *Closed Tue.* *Map 3, E9, p255* Locals will cross the entire
town for the ice-creams here, which are just that bit creamier, subtler
and naughtier than elsewhere. Highly recommended late at night.

Southwest: around via del Pratello

Restaurants

€€€ **Trattoria Battibecco**, via Battibecco 4, **T** 051-2232298.
Closed Sun. *Map 4, D2, p256* Only a trattoria by name in order to
evoke a sense of tradition, make no mistake, this is one of Bologna's most expensive and luxurious restaurants, as far away from a
trattoria as can be. The décor is sophisticated with a wooden ceiling, tiled floor and trompe l'oeil walls with backlist recesses.
There's no denying the sumptuousness of its predominantly
fish-based dishes which are mix of traditional and experimental, all
served in a refined atmosphere tucked away in a quiet narrow
street in the heart of the historic centre.

€€€ **Biagi alla Grada**, via della Grada 6, **T** 051-553025. *Closed
Tue.* *Map 2, H2, p252* Open since 1937 and still in the hands of the
founding Biagi family this traditional elegant restaurant offers typical Bolognese cuisine cooked to perfection. By common consent
the tortellini, handmade by the corpulent Signor Biagi whose size
is testament to fine living, are the best in town.

! The original recipe for Spaghetti Bolognese is a far cry from
the bastardized international version. It should contain beef,
bacon, carrots, celery, onions, tomato sauce, dry white wine,
and whole milk. The correct local name is *tagliatelle al ragu*.

€€ **Amedeo**, via Saragozza 88, **T** 051-585060, *Closed Tue.*
Map 3, D3, p254 This is a lovely restaurant with tables underneath the porticoes popular with students celebrating graduation. Amedeo is originally from Basilicata in the south of Italy but
the cuisine here is all Bolongese with one or two inventions in
the *secondi*.

€€ **Cesari**, via Carbonesi 8, **T** 051-237710. *Closed Sun, also Sat in
summer.* *Map 3, C6, p254* A warm welcome awaits here in a
resplendent inner room complete with a cast-iron chandelier and
antique engravings. The menu is a reliable, standard choice of
typical local and regional food.

Trattorie

€€ **Della Santa**, via Urbana 7, **T** 051-330415. *Closed Sun.* *Map 3,
C5, p254* Another typical Bolognese trattoria but a highlight in its
vast gastronomic landscape serving fresh home-made tortelloni
and tagliatelle in a typical arcaded building with a wood-beamed
ceiling. Nice informal service. Book ahead.

€€ **Meloncello**, via Saragozza 240, **T** 051-6143947. *Closed Mon
eve and Tue.* *Map 3, C2, p254* Superbly positioned in the corner of
the city leading out through Porta Saragozza, this old trattoria has
for years prepared those who are about to make the pilgrimage up
the porticoes to San Luca or restored them coming down. Intimate
and a little bit musty, it really feels like the extension of an Italian
family home with a dedicated clientele of regulars. The rabbit with
polenta is delicious and stuffed zucchini a speciality. Essential to
book ahead during the fesival of San Luca in May. Ask for a table in
the tiny backroom which is also non-smoking.

★ **Best** **Cheap eats**
- Grassilli, p150
- Ristorante Silverio, p150
- Trattoria Serghei, p143
- Trattoria al 15, p151
- Osteria dell'Orsa, p144

Osterie

€€ **Due Porte**, via del Pratello 62, **T** 051-523565. *Closed Tue. Map 3, A2, p254* A homely tavern serving Bolognese and southern pasta dishes with a broad selection of wines from all over Italy.

€€ **La Traviata**, via Urbana, 5/C, **T** 051-331298. *Mon-Fri for lunch. Mon-Sat for dinner. Map 3, C4, p254* Not surprisingly a musical theme reigns in this informal bar, with old instruments hung on the walls. Its low lights, dark wood and informal atmosphere as well as simple but tasty dishes make it popular with young locals.

€€ **Montesino**, via del Pratello 74, **T** 051-523426. *Closed Mon. Map 3, A2, p254* Congenial hangout for good food and wine, with a leaning towards the Sardinian roots of the owner. A quiet place as the owner will not accept groups. The poems written on the table cloths are reputedly published in a tri-annual collection.

€€ **Ribalta**, viaM d'Azeglio 41, **T** 051-331101. *Map 3, D6, p254* A charming spot with walls covered in posters of old Bologna.

€ **Bass' Otto Cafeteria**, via Ugo Bassi 8, **T** 051-232511. *Closed weekends. Map 4, C1, p256* A modern and noisy bistro ideal for a quick and inexpensive meal.

€ **Brancaleone**, via Santa Caterina 51, **T** 051-585111. *Closed Sun and Mon*. *Map 3, C3, p254* A candlelit and intimate pub-bar with a limited but tasty range of dishes from the Abruzzi region.

€ **Cantinone**, via del Pratello, 56/A, **T** 051-553223. *Closed Tue*. *Map 3, A3, p254* On a road famous for its high concentration of bars, this is one that since the 70s heyday has been popular among students and cheaper as a result. A quirky place with a broad selection of soups and wines and also just about any product you can make from milk. Not so hot on the beer.

€ **Fantoni**, via del Pratello 11 **T** 051-236358. *Closed Sun and also Mon eve*. *Map 3, A4, p254* An old-style trattoria serving very good value Bolognese food on a picturesque ancient street with views onto chiesa San Francesco and the piazza.

€ **Senzanome**, 42 via Senzannome /A, **T** 051-331147. *Closed Mon*. *Map 3, C4, p254* Delicious tripe and dishes with beans. Pleasant, simple old-world ambience, open until late.

Indian

€€ **Taj Mahal**, via San Felice 92, **T** 051-524894. *Closed Tue*. *Map 2, G2, p252* The most informal and economical of Bologna's Indian options without the attention to recreating a full-on Indian atmosphere but with typically friendly Indian service.

Cafés and gelaterie

Majani, via De' Carbonesi 5, **T** 051-234302. *Map 3, C6, p254* A Bolognese institution and the sweet equivalent of Tamburini: an elegant and mouth-watering art nouveau shrine to the city's famous chocolate-maker Signora Majani, as it was when the shop was founded in 1834. For the proverbial child in a sweet-shop.

Pielle, via San Felice 13, **T** 051-224461. *Map 2, H4, p252* All kinds of manna: liqueurs, oils, honeys and freshly ground coffee.

Ugo, via San Felice 24, **T** 051-263849. *Map 2, H4, p252* According to many locals the best gelato in town and certainly rightfully famous for high-quality creamy licks.

Northwest: around via Galliera

Restaurants

€€€ **Caracci**, via Manzoni 2, **T** 051-222049. *Mon-Sun.*
Map 4, B3, p256 This famous restaurant is located within the premises of the Grand Hotel Baglioni, the luxury address for visitors to Bologna. The restaurant itself is set in a magnificent hall with frescoes by artists from the Carracci school whose name it bears. Service is top class and the atmosphere refined, while the menu covers local specialities and also many international dishes.

€€€ **Diana**, via dell dell'Indipendenza 24, **T** 051-231302. *Closed Mon. Map 2, H7, p253* Part of the establishment since the 1920s this elegant and sophisticated restaurant, complete with crystal chandeliers is one for gourmets wanting to appreciate the finer nuances in the local cuisine. The *Dindo Diana* (turkey) and the chicken galantine are the restaurant's signature main courses while the apple meringue cake is an unmissable pudding.

€€€ **Luciano**, via N Sauro 19, **T** 051-231249. *Closed Wed. Map 2, H6, p252* Art Nouveau style restaurant, supposedly a combination of osteria and ristorante. A lovely and original place, perfect for an intimate tête-à-tête. The mellow wood interior has dimmed lighting and little alcoves for privacy. Great for a quiet lunch stop with good soups, chicken, homely pasta dishes and tempting dolci. Relatively expensive.

€€€ **Pernice e la Gallina**, via dell'Abbadia 4, **T** 051-269922. *Closed Sun. Booking compulsory for lunch Mon-Fri.*
Map 2, H3, p252 Formerly the site of an old trattoria, it has recently been kitted out with a contemporary décor that combines well with the ancient setting. The food reflects the mix of old and new. Popular with a young and sophisticated clientele. Try the roast wild duck with potatoes, apples and chestnuts.

€€ **Caminetto d'Oro**, via Falegnami 4, **T** 051-263494, www.caminettodoro.it *Closed Tue eve and Wed*. *Map 2, G7, p253* A traditional family-run restaurant next to the Arena del Sole popular with artists and actors. Meat is cooked on an open fire in winter. The menu combines the best of tradition with innovation using local and seasonal produce for maximum taste. The rigatoni with shallots and *sogliano fossa* cheese are memorable.

€€ **Il Pirata del Porto,** via del Porto 42, **T** 051-552750. *Closed Mon*. *Map 2, E5, p252* A new and popular seafood option in the upcoming former port and industrial sector of the city. Large and airy and always busy at weekends and at lunch time.

€€ **Montegrappa "da Nello"**, via Montegrappa 2, **T** 051-236331. *Closed Mon*. *Map 4, B3, p256* Despite its small entrance this is a large and cavernous restaurant which is nearly always oversubscribed. It serves very specific local dishes, according to their town of origin. A good place to witness the pride and different tastes of meats cured only kilometres away from each other.

€€ **Paranza**, piazza VII Novembre 2, **T** 051-522002. *Closed Mon*. *Map 2, E3, p252* Good value fish dishes and seafood inspired by southern Italian recipes. Not particularly exciting from outside but welcoming inside with colourful tiles.

Osterie

€€ **Da Pietro**, via Falegnami 18, **T** 051-230644. *Closed Sun except during festivals. Map 2, G7, p253* Intimately spaced tables on two floors provide for a cosy atmosphere and there are tables outside under the arcades with heaters during spring and autumn. The menu is a mixture of Umbrian and Bolognese cuisine with a small list of local wines and great puddings.

€€ **Piazza Grande**, via Manzoni 11, **T** 051-265786. *Closed Tue. Map 4, B3, p256* Open until late this osteria is popular with good-timers and gourmets. Its ancient wood-beamed ceiling makes it almost a piece of urban archaeology, adding authenticity to the delicious Emilian dishes on the menu.

€ **C'entro**, via dell'Indipendenza 45, **T** 051-234216. *Closed Sun. Map 2, G7, p253* Fast food without losing the tradition and taste. As a modern self-service canteen concept this place is very different from the majority of the city's restaurants. Popular during the week for a quick working lunch, the mass catering still retains its base in local traditions and offers a huge choice of very tasty dishes.

Chinese

€ **Fortuna**, via Morgagni 8, **T** 051-266914. *Closed Wed. Map 2, H5, p252* A well-established and respected restaurant offering typical Chiense and Vietnamese dishes in a décor to match.

Indian

€€ India, via N Sauro14, **T** 051-271095. *Closed Mon.   Map 4, B1, p256* Not your average curry house this Italian take on the Indian experience does not suffer from student stereotyping. The décor is sophisticated, detailed and well-conceived while the chefs are two Indians offering both tandoori and mughlai dishes. From Tuesday to Friday there is an excellent and highly recommended buffet lunch allowing you to taste as much as you want from a whole range of dishes for a very acceptable fixed price of €12.

Cafés

Altero, via dell'Indipendenza 33, **T** 051-234758.   *Map 2, G7, p253* One of a chain of snack bars reliable for good pizza *al taglio* (by the slice). There is also a branch at via Ugo Bassi 10, **T** 051-226612.

Calderoni, via dell'Indipendenza 70, **T** 051-248208.   *Map 2, E8 p253* A popular bar on this main street. Downstairs a range of pastas, salads and cakes are on display. In the late afternoons the upstairs turns into a piano bar serving decent cocktails and delicious ice-creams.

Duchamp Caffe d'Arte, via N Sauro 12. *Map 4, B1, p256* Very chic Parisian Art-Déco style bistro with a dark wooden interior serving select wines and beers, and a limited range of chic snacks. Expensive but cool.

Impero, via dell'Indipendenza 39, **T** 051-232337.   *Map 2, G7, p253* An old pasticceria now part of a chain but still with original furnishings serving delicious croissants and various pastries at all times.

Piccolo, via Riva Reno 114, **T** 051-236389. *Mon-Fri 1000-2000*
Map 2, G6, p252 Supposedly Bologna's first 'green' bar this place
caters for lovers of all beverages natural and organic: malt cacao,
goats milk cappuccino, plum cake with honey and many savoury
delights, organic beers, teas and tisanes.

Outskirts of Bologna

Restaurants

€€€ **Acqua Pazza**, via Murri, 168, **T** 051-443422. *Closed Sat
lunch and Mon. Southeast of centre beyond piazza Santo Stefano.*
Literally translated as 'mad water' this is an interesting and sophisticated small restaurant with more attention to modernism and
originality in décor than many of the city's restaurants. There are
water themes in the murals and the menu is one for disciples of
fish and seafood in sumptuous and surprising sauces and
preparations.

€€€ **Del Cacciatore**, via Caduti di Casteldebole 25,
T 051-564203. *Closed Sun eve and Mon. West of centre along via
Emilia Ponente then south before tangenziale.* A large, convivial and
country-style restaurant, a favourite with hunters who have
inspired its name. A long corridor leads to a vast, beamed hall with
spacious and well-spaced tables, while there are siderooms for
more privacy and non-smokers. The superb and copious menu is
predominantly game, with delicious fresh mushrooms when they
are in season, all served with local wines (from a choice of over
300) and, if you need a little help digesting, a broad range of local,
label-less grappas.

€€€ **La Bottega di Franco**, via Agucchi 112, **T** 051-311243,
F 051-388746. *Closed Mon am and Sun. West along via Emilia*

Ponente then north before river and over railway. Built at the end of the 17th century, this former country house of a Bolognese Contessa provides an elegant, secluded and bohemian setting for a romantic feast 10 minutes away by taxi from the Centro Storico. Inside the décor is bohemian and undeliberately assembled, almost Parisian with a nod to the cinema. It is no surprise that Franco organizes Murder Mystery evenings on Mondays à la Maigret. Forty people sit on one table with actors sitting among you, the plot thickening with your arteries as the evening unfolds. Otherwise the restaurant has a nice home-made feel with dishes being brought in their casseroles and then taken away as if at home. There are tables outside and Franco plans to develop the cellar downstairs. A secret it pains me to disclose. Book in advance.

€€€ **Panoramica**, via San Mamolo 31, **T** 051-580337. *Closed Sun. South through Porta San Mamolo*. Despite its slightly kitsch faux-liberty 80s décor, this is an agreeable restaurant, especially if you can sit outside on the ground floor veranda or upstairs on the terrace which is conducive to intimate conversation over a nice bottle. Big on delicious salads with mushrooms and artichokes.

€€ **Ai Butteri**, via Murri 20, **T** 051-347718. *Closed Sun. Southeast beyond Porta San Stefano*. The stereotypical Italian restaurant complete with red-checked table cloths. The cuisine is Tuscan and the gentle giant Augusto will make you feel very at home, and very full. Wash it down with a carafe of *vinsanto* and *cantucci*. It is popular and small so booking ahead is obligatory.

€€ **Boni**, via don Sturzo 22, **T** 051-6154337. *Closed Sun eve, Mon and half of Jan. Southwest along via Saragozza then fork right along via Porettana towards Casalecchio*. Old-fashioned, family-run trattoria that has been running for over 40 years, lovingly cared for by Antonio and Agnese. Simple and friendly atmosphere and wholesome home cooking.

€€ Dei Picari, via Emilia Ponente 459, **T** 051-6190367. *Closed Sat midday and Sun. West of centre beyond piazza San Felice.* A little-known gem tucked away beneath the via Emilia at the end of the Ponte Marco. Formerly a stables and coach house, the décor is typically tavern-like with assorted objects and rustic wood furnishings. The four different fixed price menus are exceptionally good value and are inclusive of wine. They offer a range of surprising takes on regional themes that attract gourmets from afar – from the sophisticated *tortelloni alle melanzane con pomodoro e mentuccia* to the basic traditional subsistence dish of the Apennine hill folk, pasta in mashed potato and garlic.

€€ Dello Sterlino, via Murri 71, **T** 051-342751. *Closed Tue. Southeast beyond piazza Santo Stefano.* Named after the starlings that used to populate this area before the city's expansion, this is a restaurant, pizzeria and hotel in one. Opened as a restaurant 80 years ago the 17th-century building was once the coach house and stopover point for travellers on their way to Florence and is alleged to have restored Goethe on his travels. Nowadays fine regional food is served to lesser mortals in a rustic setting of three arched rooms.

€€ Del Pontelungo, via Emilia Ponente 307, **T** 051-382996. *Closed Sat and Sun. Due west beyond piazza San Felice.* A historic venue as the black and white photos on the walls bear witness to. A jumbled décor of old mirrors with advertisements, modern art and old furniture. You only pay for what you drink, but that will probably be quite a lot as both the wine and the food are delicious.

€ Da Vito, via Monte Albano, 5, San Luca, **T** 051-437711. *Closed Tue. Opposite the basilica of San Luca.* At the top of the long portico this is one of the best pizzerias in town, also renowned for its choice of delicious homemade pastries and cakes, all great value and a reward for anyone who has walked up (or an inspiration to walk down for those who have not). In summer tables are also put out in the inner garden but year round the place offers spectacular views over the whole city.

€ **Paradisino**, via C Vighi 33, **T** 051-566401. *Closed Sun, also Tue except in summer. Closed Jan. West, in Reno, south off viale Palmiro Togliatti.* A wonderful old country house in a beautiful setting surrounded by green, 'the little paradise' offers excellent value open-air lunches (evening meals are usually inside) specializing in local and long-lost traditional recipes that, like most Bolognese cuisine, are not for the faint-hearted or conservationist. Try the *birichini* (little freshwater fish) or the frogs, either fried or stewed, whichever you prefer, fresh from the Reno that flows nearby.

€ **De Monte Donato,** via Siepelunga 118, **T** 051-472901. *Closed Mon. In hills beyond Giardini Margherita out of piazza Castiglione.* In the hills above the city this is a picturesque resutauarant with superb panoramic views over the city from the balcony and the second floor. A perfect and good-value summer stop-off on during weekend randonees in the countryside outside the stifling city.

Osterias

€ **Osteria Natali**, via di Casaglia 62, **T** 051-589093. *Left fork off via Saragozza to southwest.* If you are up in the surrounding hills this bar has a relaxing garden perfect for tasting a pre-dinner glass of wine with *crescentine* and salami.

African

€ **Adal**, via G Vasari 7, **T** 051-374891. *Closed Mon. In Bolognina east of via di Corticella.* An Eritrean restaurant devoted to the cuisine of one of Italy's few ex-colonies. At weekends there are often poetry readings, live African music and Ethiopia, Eritrea and Somalia films.

Cafés

La Caramella, via Cadriano 27, **T** 051-505074. *Northeast of via San Donato beyond tangenziale*. A calorifc extravaganza – one of the best cake and sweet shops in Bologna serving local specialities such as *torta di riso* (rice cake) and innovative concoctions, as well as 24 types of chocolate. At lunchtime there is a buffet of salads and piazza slices, croissants – in fact anything you could possibly want.

Poco Loco, via Mezzofanti 18, no **T**. *In a residential district south-east off via Mazzini*. A Mexican ranch-like establishment in a leafy residential area just outside the Centro Storico this is *the* place to go for brunch on Saturday mornings where a feast of abundant and delicious self-service dishes will cure any hangover.

Parma

€€€ **Parizzi**, via della Repubblica 71, **T** 0521 285952. Currently viewed as the best in town, offering a wide range of inventive and traditional dishes with impeccable service.

€€€ **Il Trovatore**, via Affo, **T** 0521 236905. Elegant and spacious, this restaurants serves up local specialties in style.

€ **Antica Osteria Fontana**, strada Farini 24, **T** 0521 286037. Mythical among locals, this authentic piece of local tradition serves inexpensive dishes and sandwiches in an atmospheric setting.

Modena

€€€ **Borso d'Este**, piazza Roma 5, **T** 059-214114. In a prime location on this magnificent square this is currently viewed as the best restaurant in town, serving adventurous and traditional dishes with equal flair and flavour – at a price.

€€€ **Cucina del Museo**, via Sant'Agostino 5, **T** 059-217429. A tiny gem in the old centre with only six tables but a big menu of creative traditional and experimental dishes. Book ahead.

€€€ **Fini**, piazzetta San Francesco, **T** 059-223314. For a long time the most renowned restaurant in town and still serving delicious food with impeccable service in a nice Art Nouveau setting.

€€ **Aldina**, via Albinelli 40. Affordable and tasty food from all over Italy.

€€ **Da Enzo**, via Coltellini 7. Modenese specialities in an old-fashioned setting. Relatively expensive.

€€ **Santa Chiara**, via Ruggera. A chic resrarurant with innovative dishes and local specialities.

€ **Giusti**, via Farini 75/vicolo Squallore 46, **T** 059-222533. Part of the furniture: a useful deli with a bar next door. Good sandwiches.

Ferrara

€€ **Antica Osteria delle Volte**, via delle Volte 37/a, **T** 0532-762033. In the medieval heart of Ferrara, this is a rustic and reasonably priced option with a good atmosphere.

€€ **Max**, piazza della Repubblica 16, **T** 0532-209309. Popular with a young crowd. Great and relatively light food with an extensive wine list.

€€ **Guido**, via Vignatagliata 6, **T** 0532-761052. Food has been served here for over 100 years. The restaurant's latest owner, Guido keeps a tradition of delicious regional specialities.

Imola

€€€ **La Volta**, via SS Selice 82, **T** 0542-5102. Refined fish specialities but also the full regional works in an Art Nouveau setting.

€€ **del Vicolo Nuovo**, vicolo Codronchi 6, **T** 0542-32552. *Closed Sun and Mon*. Traditional cuisine in a 17th-century former Jesuit school in the middle of the historic centre.

€€ **San Domenico**, vicolo Sacchi 1. *Closed Sun eve and Mon*. Considering the fact that this restaurant is considered one of the best in all Italy it is amazing you don't have to have won the lottery to afford to eat here. Should be your first port of call.

Rimini

€€ **Marinelli da Vittorio**, viale Valurio 39, **T** 0541-783289. Fun and busy restaurant in the centro storico. Great fresh fish.

€€ **Saraghina's**, via Poletti 32, **T** 0541-783794. Superior seafood in a cordial central setting.

€ **Acero Rosso**, viale Tiberio 11, **T** 0541-53577. Elegant with courtyard in summer in the old centre.

Bologna has a kicking bar and club scene. Ever since the city became a university centre its students have needed to be entertained, distracted from their studies and inspired by alcoholic hedonism and hallucination. The drinking traditions of Bologna's down-at-heel osterie goes back almost a thousand years and they are still intact now even if the venues themselves have gone a little more upmarket. Add to that historic vibrancy a present-day openness and an ability to absorb and experiment with new influences and you have a city that is more unchained than most in Italy. Music and original hybrid bar-cum-nightclub experiences to suit most tastes, persuasions and moods are on offer. A number of Bologna's clubs attract international names on the DJ circuit. Activity centres around two or three areas, kicking off the evening in the Quadrilatero, piazza Minghetti or piazza Malpighi before the ritual of supper after which the crowds move on to the concentration of bars in either the university district or around via del Pratello.

Aperitivo time (1900-2100) is when everyone gets going, drinking tiny multi-coloured cocktails, or *prosecco* and snacking on a wide selection of free nibbles that every bar provides. Then it's dinner time which stretches until around 2300, when you can again change venue for a *digestivo* (after dinner drink).

Most of the innovative and edgy nightclubs are in the northwest of the city and just outside, while more traditional, boppy discos are to be found in the surrounding hills. Bars with English names are generally to be avoided. Some bars and clubs legally have to belong to social circles and you may be asked for a *tessera* (membership card) for one of the social clubs (eg ARCI). Usually if you say you are just visiting and leave some ID at the door you won't have to buy the membership which otherwise costs around €20-30 for a year. Clubs that don't require membership usually charge around €10-15. This generally includes an obligatory (alcoholic) drink. For a comprehensive listing of bars and nightclubs and for up to date information on who or what's on where, consult the excellent *TalkaBOut* English language monthly or the new bi-lingual monthly magazine published by the commune, BOnews.

Centre: piazza Maggiore and around

Bars

Al Calice, via Clavature 13, **T** 051-264506. *Closed Sun Map 4, E5, p256* A modern, neutral-looking bar specializing in fresh oysters at aperitif time, together with the appropriate tipple.

Café De Paris, piazza Minghetti, **T** 051-234980. *Open daily until late. Map 4, F5, p256* This is the hottest night-spot at the moment and also does great lunches. At night there are masses of top *aperitivi* snacks, plates of pasta, sandwiches, crisps, olives – which means it is packed between 1900 and 2100 on Fridays and

★ **Clavature aperitivos**

Fashionable Bolognesi swarm into the cafés of the Quadrilatero at aperitivo time, spilling out onto the narrow streets.

Saturdays when the beautiful people come to cruise and the DJ cranks up the volume. Things calm down later and you can find a table in the covered outdoor section.

Canton de' Fiori, via dell'Indipendenza 1, **T** 051-267300. *Closed Sun. Map 4, C3, p256* In the ancient quadrivio where the florists sell their fragrant wares with a few tables outside under porticoes in summer season. Frescoes above the entrance depict three goods bestowed by mother nature on man: bread, wine and canapa with the inscription *in vina laetitia e cannabis protecta*.

Mocambo, via d'Azeglio 1/7, **T** 051-229 516. *0700-2030. Closed Sun. Map 4, E3, p256* Aperitifs for the chic with delicious spicy nibbles and generous glassfuls of your favourite plonk. Also do fantastic breakfasts with the famed, super creamy, *café crème*.

Rosa Rose, via Clavature 18, **T** 051-225071. *Map 4, E5, p256* At its quietest at lunch but still popular for a light snack, this place transforms at night with great crowds of sunglassed *fighetti* spilling out onto the narrow street with the gigantic appetizers on offer at aperitivo time. So varied and bountiful are they that you'll be hard-pushed to leave with an appetite afterwards. Currently one of Bologna's trendiest night-spots (you're either a Café de Paris or a Rosa Rose person) the bar is jam-packed in the evenings and the locals fall over themselves to be seen here. Take one of the laden carving boards and sit more peacefully in the street.

Northeast: the university quarter

Bars

Birreria Il Druido, via Mascarella 26/b, **T** 051-226757. *Closed Wed. Map 2, G10, p253* More than 150 brands of beer with good sandwiches and chatty bartenders. Open air seating during the hot summer months.

Bottega del Vino Olindo Faccioli, via Altabella 15, **T** 051-223171. 1800-0200. *Closed Sun. Map 4, C4, p256* Recently restored this historic and centrally located tavern still retains its 1920s interior with dark wood furnishings, stylish chairs and the main bar area. A convivial place for the evening aperitif where in theory, in time-honoured ritual, the first drink should contain an uovo sodo (boiled egg) – not obligatory. Wine tasting evenings are organized occasionally.

Cantina Bentivoglio, via Mascarella 4/b, **T** 051-222 119. *From 2000. Closed Mon. Map 2, G9, p253* The heart of the Bolognese night-scene, this huge cavernous jazz café offers great wine and simple food and live jazz every night. The specials are always worth checking and are delicious. You can chose to sit down by the band and pay a little extra, or stick to the quieter rooms on ground level. Booking is essential for a Sat-night table downstairs.

Celtic Druid, via Caduti di Cefalonia 5, **T** 051-224 212. *Open daily. Just off via Rizzoli.* *Map 4, G10, p253* An Irish Pub with a name one would never find on the Esmerald Isle, but it does boast Irish staff and a happy hour from opening at 2030. This is the first port of call for ex-pat workers and the kind of place where everyone remembers your name.

Cluricaune, via Zamboni 18, **T** 051-263419. *Just around the corner from the Hotel San Donato.* *Map 4, B7, p256* This Irish bar is more Irish than most you find in Ireland. But its vaulted ceilings and rickety wooden furnishings and barrels (unusually unkempt for Italy) do a good job of creating a dark and smokily traditional atmosphere. It is usually packed, mostly with students and the atmosphere is kicking. A good place to mix with the young locals, watch sport on TV and for the homesick to enjoy a good pint of Guinness.

Contavalli, via Belle Arte, 2, **T** 051-268 395. *Closed Sun.* *Map 2, H9, p253* Odd but fun little *aperitivo* bar with art shows every so often. They also serve *bruschetta* and snacks in the back room.

Da Matusel, via Bertoloni 2, **T** 051-231718. *Closed Sat lunchtime and Sun.* *Map 2, G10, 253* Meaning 'Mad Bird' this is a popular and noisy bar near the university.

Insomnia, via de'Giudei 8, **T** 051-261552. *Closed Mon.* *Map 4, C6, p256* Trendy bar open until late with outdoor seating in the summer.

Hollywood Party, via Goito, **T** 051-233199. *Open late.* *Map 4, A4, p256* Groovy bar attracting the cool and the cross-dressing crowd though the venue is a gay/straight mix.

L'Antica Stuzzicheria, via Mascarella, no **T**. *Map 2, G9, p253* Crammed full of interesting odds and ends and with extremely genial staff, this is a bar full of dark intimate corners for clandestine jugs of wine and plates of cheese with your *amore*.

Moodys, via Mascarella, 84/b, **T** 051-249510. *Open until late. Map 2, F10, p253* With happy hour prices from 2100-2330 you can't go far wrong for strong cocktails and loud music, with a restaurant round the back in case you find you just can't leave.

Rose Selavy, via Marsala 5, **T** 051-271961. *Map 2, B7, p253* Super-chic restaurant/bar. Everything about this bar screams Lenny Kravitz from the zebra-print upholstery to the 'is that a small creature?' light shades. A place to see and be seen, with famously slow service.

Bistrot Le Stanze (del Tenente), via Borgo San Pietro 1, **T** 051-228767. *Closed Sun and Sat lunchtime. Map 2, G9, p253* Set in the magnificent former chapel of the Bentivoglio, with tall stone ceilings and walls covered in 17th-century frescoes, this bar has one the city's most unusual, edgy and creative décors, very popular with young and trendy locals. Onto this classical background the owners have placed a mixture of futuristic, Gothic and 70s furnishings, from tall dribbled candlesticks, to metal lamps and orange sofas. There are three contrasting rooms off the main bar, each divided by a secretive curtain. One is a dining room with a traditional menu served in trendy (small) portions. If its not taken, sit on the raised section where the altar used to be. The venue sometimes hosts classical music concerts. Cocktails are the speciality of the house. Internet.

Lord Lister, via Zamboni 56, **T** 051-240886. *Map 2, H11, p253* A lively English-style pub under the porticoes of the student district with ranch-like sets of tables and chairs outside.

X, via del Borgo di San Pietro. *Map 2, F9, p253* Very *fighetto* Cuban, Latin-America bar.

Scuderia, piazza Verdi. *Map 4, B8, p256* Recently opened, this bar-club under a beautiful frescoed arch stands on the site of the former stables (*scuderia*) of the Bentivoglio family. Run by the Rosa Rose group it is a typically funky hybrid of cool grooves and tunes for young, trendy and beautiful locals. Occasionally hosts concerts and live music on the square outside.

Lido del Guasto, via del Guasto, www.universointerculturale.it *Map 4, A8, p256* Literally meaning 'waste' the 'guasto' is a regenerated former children's playground built in 1970s which had been lost to drug pushers. A manifestation of the creativity of the Bolognese youth, this bar hosts a free-wheeling and apparently improvized mix of post-modern fashion shows, art shows, and a changing choice of music from piano-bar relaxation to drum 'n' bass, all in the open air.

Marsalino, via Marsala, 13/d, **T** 051-238 675. *Closed Mon, 1200-0200. Map 4, B7, p256* Cosy café with great specials and good wine. Very small so get there early.

Clubs

Kinki, via Zamboni 1, **T** 051-268935. *Map 4, C6, p256* Designer kitsch and fusion funk and house for gay and beautiful straight people. Mirrors and vinyl décor under the Two Towers. One of *the* places, especially in spring.

Corto Maltese, via del Borgo di San Pietro 9, **T** 051-229746. *Daily until 0400. Map 4, G9, p253* Disco pub with a little something for everyone. Sam's happy hour goes from 1930-2100 with Milanese-style *apperitivi* in the form of huge free plates of pasta. The back room starts pumping up the volume at around 2200, and a mixed crowd of students and young professionals come to drink cocktails, play pool and dance the night away.

Soda Pops, via Castel Tialto 6, **T** 051-272 079. *Off via San Vitale. Map 4, D6, p256* Funky dungeonesque bar/club by the Two Towers with free entrance until late. Popular with students for its super-strength cocktails, the music has lately veered towards US rap.

Jam Club, via Mascarella, 2a, **T** 051-221003. *Map 2, H9, p253* Much less of a student hang-out with Monday-night-is- rock-night for an over 25 crowd. Generally women get in free before 0100, and the men have to pay all night. With a small restaurant catering for midnight munchies, this is also one of the few clubs that sells cigarettes.

Zoom, via Mascarella 60, **T** 051-241963. *Map 2, F10, p253* Tiny mixed gay/straight bar with occasional live music, and 'park' nights, where the bar is transformed with turf, branches, flowers and starlight into an indoor-outdoor kind of thing. Different.

Southeast: Santo Stefano and around

Bars

Alla Corte di Bacco, corte Isolani 7, **T** 051-237884. *Map 4, E7, p256* In the arcade complex just off piazza Santo Stefano this is a lovely little wine bar offering over 400 different labels.

Chalet Giardini Margherita, Giardini Margherita **T** 051-307593. *Open every day in summer. Map 3, G11, p255* This bar/café in the centre of the park by the lake is an excellent venue for watching the sun go down over an ice-cream or something a little stronger.

Godot Wine Bar, via Cartoleria 12, **T** 051-226315 (and **Godot Wine Store** on via Santo Stefano, 12, **T** 051-26187). *0800-0200, Closed Sun. Just before the seven churches. Map 3, G11, p255* This wine bar boasts a broad range of top wines and a range of delicate little dishes to accompany them. Open almost all day, it is a great alternative for a good breakfast, lunch, light supper or for a tipple after the theatre. Service is quick despite the bar's name.

Maurizio, via Guerrazzi, 22/A. *Closed Sun*. Map 3, D9, p255 Small cosy bar packed with antique radios and Bolognese sporting memorabilia – mostly from the two local basketball teams Fortitudo and Virtus. A live jazz venue every Friday night, the bar is also open all day for budget sandwiches and snacks.

Taberna dei Frati, via Arienti 25, **T** 051-23 98 80. *Open late*. Map 3, E8, p255 Good for a quiet drink last thing in a street away from the bustle of the centre. Broad selection of beers and tasty panini.

Vicolo, via Sampieri 3. Map 4, D6, p256 Typically inventive hybrid of bar, cinema and nightclub, with thematic evening every Wednesday celebrating different countries and cultures. There is a happy hour from 1900-2200 with cocktails, buffet of the featured cuisine and an original language movie. The music takes over at 2200. Entrance free to tourists or students on these days. For the programme of events check www.serateinternazionali.it

Clubs

Baraccano, viale Gozzadini, (opposite the Giardini Margherita) **T** 051-301211. *Open Jun-Sep*. Map 3, F11, p255 Two or three stages provide the venue for bands and entertainers in this private park, with tables and chairs spread out under the huge old pine trees and two bars.

Ex Porto di Mare, via Sampieri 3, **T** 051-224256. *Closed Mon. Behind the Due Torri*. Map 4, D6, p256 Live bands at weekends and Greek food in basement.

Southwest: around via del Pratello

Bars

All'Inzu, via del Pratello 5a. *Closed Sun.* *Map 3, A4, p254* Trendy bar with big screen.

Caracol, piazza Galileo, 6, **T** 051-222 610. *Until 0200.* *Map 4, E2, p256* Mexican bar/restaurant with excellent pitchers of Margarita and a very small dance floor. Happy hour 1930-2030.

Circolo Pavese, via del Pratello 51/3, **T** 051-550221. *Closed Sun. Until 0300.* *Map 3, A3, p254* Access only with the ARCI (see p171) passcard (purchasable on site) this is a place to go to sip wine to a backdrop of experimental theatre and short film projections in the company of Bologna's would-be artists.

Far Magia, via S Isaia, 4/bc, **T** 051-6449561. *Map 3, B4, p254* Packed and pricey cocktail bar with great decor and a good chef offering a delicious and daily varying menu. Look out for the girl in a silver bikini on a swing and the dancing Chinese dragon.

Habana Vieja, via de Grifoni, 5/2, **T** 051-584313. *1900-late.* *Map 4, F1, p256* Cocktails, Mexican tapas, Cuban cigars – this place is Latino overload but fun. Thursdays is live music with visiting 'Cuban' bands. Lively at weekends. This is also the safest bar in Bologna due to the proximity of the *Questura,* so if you have a taste for off-duty boys in blue who know how to *Lambada*, this is heaven.

Kappa Sushi, piazza Malpighi, 14, **T** 051-221 773. *Map 3, A4, p254* Bar/restaurant offering cool relief from daily madness. Water pours from ceiling to floor in a constant stream, while mellow lounge tunes from resident DJs soothe the soul. Slip by for a

Japanese beer or full set menu amongst the foliage. Booking is essential as the bar gets busy with *Beat Party* on Saturdays, gay night on Tuesdays and international DJs the rest of the time. Spontaneous chair dancing is highly probable as the small hours approach.

Monastero, via del Pratello, 66/a, **T** 051-557172. *Closed Sun. Map 3, A3, p254* Huge arched wooden doors and killer cocktails, this is an upmarket little spot to stop and have a natter. Outdoor seating in summer.

Riff Raff, via del Pratello 3, **T** 051-222888. *Open until the last person leaves. Closed Mon. Map 3, A4, p254* A pleasant wine bar with a good selection of international labels and good salads, cold meats and cheeses too. Also mouth-watering Sicilian puddings with half-bottles of dessert wine to accompany them.

Rovescio, via Pietralata 75, **T** 051-523545. *2000-0200. Closed Mon. Map 2, H2, p252* Owned by the Greek owner of To Steki, this wine bar has an international flavour both in its wines and small hot meals which are served until 0230. A useful place late at night and a nice little place for a quiet drink with friends.

Stranamore, via del Pratello 44a. *Map 3, A3, p254* Achingly trendy but with occasional art shows.

Transilvania Horror Kafe, via San Felice 134, **T** 051-556 444, (there's also a branch on via Zamboni). *Map 2, G2, p252* 3-D version of Meatloaf's *Bat out of Hell* album cover. Red lighting, shelve-loads of skulls and clear glass table-coffins complete with skeletons and the occasional snake. Interesting.

Viola, via Sant'Isia, 24, T 051-331 884. *Closed Thu, open 1700-2300. Map 3, B3, 254* Gentle Austrian-style café and one of the few places in town with seats and plenty of space to stretch tired legs. Also do great *aperitivi*, but close early.

Walkabout, via Nosadella. *Map 3, C5, p254* New happening bar very close to the English language cinema. Full of bright young things from the early evening onwards, there is also a quieter room out the back for those just wanting a drink and a chat.

Zelig, via Porta Nuova, 4/b (off piazza Malpighi) **T** 051-236737. *Map 3, A4, p254* Open every day for drinks or supper, this is the favourite hangout of Marco Jaric, the local basketball star. Run by a charismatic *signora* with unusual taste in clothing. Book ahead.

Clubs

Blade Runner, via S. Isaia 57d. *Closed Tue. Map 3, A2, p254* Discobar with downstairs dancefloor. Favourite with trendy locals.

Cabaret Voltaire, via Saragozza 15, **T** 051-6448426. *Map 3, C4, p254* Live music and dancing to various music according to the weekly menu.

Depot Hip Hop Gallery, via del Pratello 13a. *Closed Sun. Map 3, A4, p254* Dark, atmospheric designer bar with live DJ, art gallery and small dance floor. Gay on Tuesday.

HypeClub, via Santa Margherita, 7/2, **T** 340-3346980. *2230-0300. Closed Sun. Entrance fee. Map 4, E1, p256* Recent renovation has turned this popular venue into the hottest club in town. Mondays see cheap drinks for students and foreigners, Tuesdays are rock-nights with 80's classics, and Fridays are for funksters with the Sole Shaker parties: well-known Mellow Yellow DJs spinning the latest Italian grooves.

Northwest: around via Galliera

Bars

Auld Dubliner, via Cairoli, 2/c, **T** 051-243138. *Open lunch and evenings. Map 2, E6, p252* Large, spacious and friendly, this is the only venue in town (possibly in Italy) to offer genuine UK favourites such as shepherd's pie, fish and chips and baked potatoes with chilli. With an all-Irish bar staff this is the place to drown your sorrows in pints of ice-cold Guinness.

Borderline, via Riva di Reno, 110, **T** 051-221359. *1200-1500, 1830-0230. Closed Tue. Map 2, G6, p252* Large friendly bar offering happy hour priced drinks between 1830 and 2130, with a fantastic array of *aperitivi* snacks. They also have a full range of board-games out the back and are happy for you to while away the hours over a pint and a game of backgammon.

Chet Baker, via Polese 7/a, **T** 051-22 37 95, www.chetbaker.com *Closed Sun. Map 2, G6, p252* Jazz café with indoor seating and a veranda in the summer. Open for lunch with Emilian cuisine, worth booking ahead. Mussolini's son has been known to play this venue with a host of *fascisti* packing the place out in advance.

Del Mercato, via Belvedere 13, **T** 051-237844. *Map 4, C3, p256* Opposite the *mercato delle Erbe*, a nice place to relax with a lunchtime glass of wine after the bustle of shopping.

Rumba, via Milazzo 17/f, **T** 051-63 90 792, www.rumbacafe.it *Map 2, E7, p253* Modern and trendy resto-café with live jazz and blues on Wednesdays. Happy 'hour' on Thursday from 1800-2330. The menu boasts a range of international and fusion cooking, different from the traditional regional dishes.

Clubs

Cassero (ex Salara), via Don Minzoni, **T** 051-649 44161.
www.cassero.it *From 2300. Map 2, E3, p252* This male gay club
has moved underground to the docks and vaults where the city's
salt supply used to be unloaded and stored. Currently the coolest
cavern in town for all persuasions, serving up a changing mix of
house, fusion, and lounge funk. If only for its intriguing architecture and history the place demands to be checked out. With café,
bookshop and beautiful roof garden plus views.

Kaos, via San Carlo 12, **T** 051-239964. *Map 2, F6, p252* An old, traditional feature of Bologna's night scene. Disco and techno music.
Circolo ARCI (see p171).

Link, via Fioravanti 14. *10 minutes on foot behind the train station.*
www.linkproject.org **T** 051-370971. *0000 – early hours. Free except
for specific gigs and big International DJs. Map 2, C2, p252* Ultra-
funky *centro sociale* in a converted multi-storey carpark with
futuristic bar upstairs and enormous dance floor downstairs.
Performance art and live bands moving to techno later.

Millennium, via Riva Reno, 77a. *Map 2, G5, p252* Fun, dark venue
hosting art shows and diverse live music from French accordion
players to little-known UK funk DJs. Happy hour before 2130.

Spazio alato, via Lame 2, **T** 051-227940. *Map 2, H4, p252* Nightclub and exhibition space hybrid with one-off events.

Outskirts of Bologna

Bars

Birreria Amadeus, via G Dagnini 1, **T** 051-6234011. *Southeast of Centro Storico*. Over 100 types of beers from German lagers to strong Belgian beers and including exotic brews from New Zealand and Japan. Pizza slices, crostini and pastries are complimentary munchies. A little more expensive than most bars.

Enoteca Vini d'Italia, via Emilia Levante 142, **T** 051-541509. *Closed Sun. Southeast of Centro Storico*. The place to go if you are a wine connoisseur (or even a pretendu) and want to taste the full range of Italy's vast (and sometimes besmirched) choice of wines, interspersed by bites of salami, cheese and crescentine.

Kik Bar, via San Donato, **T** 051-511328. *Northeast of Centro Storico*. Prides itself on being the bar where you can taste every possible type and label of whisky on the face of the earth.

Clubs

Estragon Balera Ska, via Giambologna 4, **T** 051-365825, www.estragon.it *Wed, Fri and Sat 2100-dawn. Concerts start at 2200. East of centre, off via Massarenti*. Serves cocktails, sangria, wine, and loads of beers. Live ska, reggae and hardcore USA, popular with the student crowd. Famously hosted Gomez when they were in town, so worth checking the programme.

Covo, viale Zagabria, **T** 051-508801, www.covoclub.com In the 'lounge bar and disco' category this club is best known for the international flavour of the live sets with groups and DJs from the US and all over Europe performing a fun mix of '80's and indie stuff.

Acquaria Club, via S Zampieri 2, **T** 051-6310801. Cabaret and live music.

Ruvido, via Maserati 9, **T** 051-6311892. *In the hillls due south of centre out of piazza San Mamolo.* Popular with the *fighetti* (the well-heeled crowd) this club and restaurant hosts 70's and 80's funk on Wednesdays, dance and cover bands on Fridays and 'Supergroove' on Saturdays – with other live concerts every night. Big dance floor.

La Lumiera, via Sabbiuno 4, **T** 051-589182. *Summer club. Due south of centre en route to Sabbiuno.* Organized by the Rosa Rose group (Rose Selavy etc), this is essentially *fighetto* fun in the hills when the going gets hot in town.

Villa Serena, via della Barca, 1, **T** 051-6156789. Country villa close to *Lo Stadio* (an inexpensive taxi ride away) open at weekends with tables and chairs under the trees, free entry and cheap drinks. The top floor is home to art shows and installations , the ground floor has two bars with 80s-90s music. The basement has live local music until midnight, and dancing to poppy stuff until 0300.

La Corte degli Aranci, via Dozza, 26 San Lazzaro, **T** 051-451541. *Summer disco, closed Sun. Bus 27 or 19 from via Rizzoli towards San Lazzaro. Look out for the big sign on the left. Restaurant opens at 2000, booking is essential.* Dancing starts at 2230 and goes on 'til 0330. Well-heeled crowd.

Villa Montefano, via Volpino, 13 Budrio, **T** 051-6929587, www.montefano.com *Northwest of centre out through piazza San Felice.* Booking is essential, as is a car. This 17th-century frescoed *palazzo* plays host to various classical, jazz and opera concerts, with the entrance price and membership card covering all the wine you can drink, and a light supper after the music.

Livello 57, via Muggia 6, **T** 051-271066. Italian version of a squat with jungle, reggae and ragamuffin. Bands occasionally plus pizzas next door. Popular with the student crowd.

Palazzo dei Congressi, piazza Cosituzione 5 , **T** 051-637 5165. *In the Fiera district.* Concert venue. Tickets from Minella Rock Shop, via Mazzini 146.

Studios, via Massarenti 14. *East of centre (bus 11).* Bands and dancing plus screening of art films. ARCI (see p171) members only.

Modena

Vox, viale Vittorio Veneto, 13 41015 Nonantola, Modena, www.voxclub.it The best venue around for big name bands such as Coldplay, Morrissey and Suede. Book in advance over the web or at the ticketmasters in town.

Rimini

Rimini's clubs are famed for their size, international DJs and the outrageous show-dressing of their core clients.

Paradiso, via Covignano 260. Dance music with famous international DJs.

Bandiera Gialla, via Covignano. Open air raving in summer only.

Pascia (Riccione), via Sardegna 30. Garage, techno and house Italian-style.

Cocorico (Riccione), via Chieti 44. Italian techno in a glass pyramid.

Bologna has a thriving arts scene fuelled by budding and aspiring student artists and a very supportive local council. Particularly around the university district, the city is plastered with posters announcing the latest show, event or spectacle and flyers are constantly handed to you along via Belle Arti, via Zamboni and via dell'Indipendenza. An excellent TimeOut-style monthly English guide, TalkaBOut (www.talkabout.it) available in many hotels, bars, bookshops and cinemas has reviews of bars, restaurants and exhibitions in the city. There are free local Italian newspapers, *CityBologna*, *BolognaBologna* and *Leggo Bologna* which provide space for and actively promote youth art. The council has also just started published a monthly bi-lingual guide to the city's arts entitled *Bonews*. The Bolognese are also very talented at improvising and converting the most surprising urban spaces into exhibition venues, be they car parks, wastelands or disused buildings. Many of the city's churches, virtually art galleries themselves, often host temporary exhibitions and concerts.

Cinema

Bologna has several **art house cinemas** and cineclubs showing films in the original language, sometimes with and sometimes without subtitles.

Fulgor, via Montegrappa 2, **T** 051-231325.
Lumiere, via Pietralata 55a. Film club with classics in their original version, www.cinetecadibologna.it
Odeon, via Mascarella 3, **T** 051-227916.

There are also plenty of **mainstream cinemas** showing the latest blockbusters. Tickets usually cost around €7, around €5 for concessions. In addition there are often many short film projections in bars and as part of sound and light spectacles.

Imperiale, via dell'Indipendenza 6, **T** 051-223732.
Medusa, viale Europa 5, 051 6300511, www.medusacinema.it
Marconi, via Saffi 58, **T** 051-6492374.

English Language Cinema

Mondays at **Cinema Nosadella**, via Nosadella 21, **T** 051-331506 and **Cinema Embassy**, via Azzogardino 61 **T** 051-555563 and Thursdays at **Tiffany**, piazza Porta Saragozza 55a, 051 523812.

Comedy

As befits a rebellious city, Bologna has a long-standing tradition of satire, practiced and honed to a fine art on so many Lords and Popes. Bologna is the head office of Italy's only satirical newspaper, *Cuore*, a weekly rag of irreverence similar to *Private Eye*. There is no long-standing tradition of stand-up comedians in Italy and comedy is usually acted out within plays and spectacles on show at one of the city's theatres. The closest thing to Italian stand-up is at **Ruvido**, east of town at via Maserati 9, **T** 051-6311892. One

Emilia-Romagna was birthplace to many famous Italian directors such as Bernardo Bertolucci and Antonio Antonioni. Most famous however is probably Federico Fellini, born in Rimini. His film *Amarcord* is a nostalgic account of and inspired by his childhood in Rimini.

the city's current most acerbic and satirical voices is that of the novelist, journalist and playwright, Stefano Benni.

Music

Bologna has a fine and long-standing tradition in both classical music, as the place where musicians such Rossini, Verdi and Respighi studied and composed, and popular music as the home-town of old-time rockers, Lucio Dalla and Vasco Rossi, Italian equivalents of Elton John and David Bowie at least in terms of longevity.

Teatro Comunale, largo Respighi 1, **T** 051-529011/051-529999 www.comunalebologna.it Bologna's famous main concert hall for classical recitals and operas. Very smart.

Rock concerts are held at the city's football stadium, **Stadio R Dall'Ara**, via A Costa 174 and at the Parco Nord in the Fiera district. Bologna is usually one of the big venues on tours of national and international artists.

In recent years Bologna has also become a centre for jazz, attracting residences by many international jazz names: **La Cantina Bentivoglio**, via Mascarella 4, **T** 051-265416 (see also Eating p173); **Chet Baker**, via Polese 7/a, **T** 051-22 37 95, closed Sun, www.chetbaker.com; **Container Club**, via dello Stallo 7, **T** 051-5311986; **Estragon**, via Calzoni 6, **T** 051-365825 – reggae, ragamuffin and ska.

Arts and entertainment

★ The Leaning Tower of Bologna
*Local legend has it that the angle of the Torre Garisenda was a delib-
erate ploy by a lover wanting to be nearer the object of his desires. In
actual fact it started to lurch due to subsidence in the 14th century.*

Theatre

Italians have a great tradition of theatre which it seems they live out in their daily lives as they talk. Bologna has a broad range of theatres hosting all types of performance from the traditional classics of Goldoni, via the modern plays of Pirandello through to experimental and abstract theatre and comedies. The city attracts productions with star-studded Italian casts and also provides a stage for its own budding writers, directors and actors.

Teatro Alemanni, via Mazzini 65, **T** 051-303609, www.clubdiapason.org   This theatre specializes in shows in the Bolognese dialect or by local actors and writers.

Teatro Arena del Sole, via dell'Indipendenza 44, **T** 051-270790. Classic Italian plays, usually from 17th-19th centuries.

Teatro Celebrazioni, via Saragozza 234, **T** 051-6153370. Hip venue for Italian plays and musicals as well as some international hits such as Grease and Rocky Horror.

Teatro Dehon, via Libia 59, **T** 051-342934.

Teatro delle Moline, via delle Moline 1, **T** 051-235288, www.teatrodellemoline.it   Modern, experimental and abstract Italian theatre in a cool surrounding.

Teatro Duse, via Cartoleria 42, **T** 051-225284/226606. Shows concentrating on local history and culture and abstract 20th-century theatre.

Teatro San Leonardo, via San Vitale 63, **T** 051-232280/234822. A 'laboratory' for experimental theatre which also stages occasional classical and light music recitals.

Teatro Testoni, via Matteotti 16, **T** 051-377790. Shows for and including children.

La Soffitta, Centro di Promozione Teatrale, via Barbiera 4, **T** 051-2092021, www.muspe.unibo.it/soffitta   Modern and alternative cinema, dance, theatre and concert shows and workshops.

Celebrating generally has always been important for the Bolognese, as befits a people who regard every meal as a feast and who were never shy about celebrating their independent spirit at each overthrow of a Pope, tyrannical lord or invader. Any victory and its anniversary was a licence to throw a party and on such occasions in medieval times the streets would fill with jesters and revelers. Jousts would take place and Bologna even had its own *palio*, a horse race, similar to that which still runs in Siena, around the piazza Maggiore. The race, organized by San Bartolomeo, took place on August 24th every year in order to commemorate the capture and bringing to Bologna of Re Enzo, son of Frederick II, after the Battle of Fossalta. Another famous festival was *la festa della porchetta*, held on the same day, involving food and finally a suckling pig being thrown down on the masses as a gift by the nobility from the window of the Palazzo Comunale. Napoleon failed to see the funny side of either festival and banned both upon commencing his occupation of Bologna.

Nowadays, though still generally festive, Bologna's main festivals are those which follow the peaks of the religious calendar (Ascension, Carnival etc), though there are also some artistic festivals organized by the council.

February

Carnevale Bologna's carnival belongs to its children who usually take part in a masked parade.

May

Festa di San Luca Bologna's main festival. On Ascension Day a procession accompanies the icon of San Luca down along the magnificent colonnade from its sanctuary on the hill, through the Porta Saragozza and eventually to the Cathedral of San Pietro. Here the icon lies in state for a week, during which time a series of powerful masses are held, before it is then returned to its home.

Matricole Today only an insipid echo of the animated and lewd 19th-century student initiation rituals.

Addobbi This ceremony, which has lost its medieval richness, takes place every Sunday in May and June. In celebration of the arrival of the Eucharist procession the city's churches adorn themselves and the streets in colourful drapes and lights.

Palio di San Giorgio (Ferrara) On the last Sunday in May, a medieval parade and horserace in the city centre.

June

Feste della Laurea Graduating is a seriously big deal in Italy. There are no city-wide graduation ceremonies, but you are sure to know about it if you find yourself in a restaurant of recent graduates.

July

Festivale dell'Estate (Modena) A mid-July week of festivities, including parades and extra-special meals, in honour of Este family.

July-August

Bologna Sogna or **Viva Bologna** This summer arts festival was recently initiated in order to stimulate the city in the summer when much of the population escapes either to the coast or the mountains. Open-air cinema and subsidized shows of all types go on all over the city and a temporary stage is put up in piazza Maggiore.

November

Baccanale (Imola) A Dionysian and calorific feast of special menus, tastings and general indulgence.

December

Natale (25th) As in most of Italy, Christmas consists of a family meal focused around roast lamb.

Vecchione (31st) The advent of the New Year is hailed by the burning of the old one, a ragdoll effigy which is set alight on the stroke of midnight in piazza Maggiore to the sound of crackers.

Bologna is a shopper's paradise for everything from food and clothes to antiques, bric-a-brac and hats. Not surprisingly for a university town, it is also well-stocked with bookshops. All of Italy's famous fashion designers and of course the local firms such as La Perla and Furla have typically stylish branches here, with prices still cheaper than outside Italy. And if you want to bottle some of the amazing tastes you've been feasting on in Bologna's restaurants there are plenty of delis and food shops for all tastes and waists.

Retail therapists should head for the via M d'Azeglio, via Farini and the catwalk-like Galleria Cavour arcade off Farini. Gourmets will have eyes bigger than their wallets and suitcases in the market streets of the Quadrilatero off piazza Maggiore.

Shopping hours are normally 0930-1300 and 1530-2000. Shoppers resident outside the European Union can claim tax refunds on their purchases. For more information on how to do, this contact Global Refund, www.taxfree@it.globalrefund.com

Alternative

Mondo Bizzarro, piazza San Martino 3, **T** 051-229737. Books, videos and magazines relating to trash culture: fetish, occult, S&M, drugs… a taste of rebellious Bologna.

Inde le Palais, via Marchesana 2. The coolest shop in town, set in the fortifications around piazza Maggiore. Clothes, furniture and various Indiana – like an Indian version of London's Momo, with the seat of Bologna's hyper-cool Fashion Radio station churning out grooves in the basement to the slogan "Love the past. Kiss the future."

Antique shops

You will find many, mostly quite expensive and stuffy antique shops along via San Vitale and via Santo Stefano.

Freak Ando, via delle Moline 14, **T** 051-271404. *Map 2, H9, p253*
20th-century collectibles: Art Déco, Biedermeier, Liberty in a real shop of curiosities.

Books

Libreria delle Moline, via delle Moline 3, **T** 051-232053. *Map 2, H9, p253* New and old books, favoured by students and bookworms.

Libreria di Cinema Teatro Musica, via Mentana 1, **T** 051-237277. *Map 4, A6, p256* Specialist in performing arts books.

Libreria Feltrinelli, piazza di Porta Ravegnana 1, **T** 051-261392. Main branch of Italy's largest and best bookstore chain.

Libreria Feltrinelli Internazionale, via Zamboni 7,
T 051-268210. *Map 4, C6, p256* Just next door, stocking English
books and books in their original languages.

Itinerari, via San Vitale 51, **T** 051-2960471. *Map 3, B11, p255*
A quiet and well-stocked travel bookshop, also with some travel
equipment.

Libreria antiquaria Palmaverde, via dei Poeti 4, **T** 051-232085.
Second-hand and antique book shop, a favourite with writers.

Libreria Feltrinelli, via dei Mille 12, **T** 051-240302. *Map 2, F7,
p253* Branch of the nationwide chain, also open late at night.

Clothing

Without listing them all, the local outlets of Italy's **fashion design-
ers** are to be found in the roads off piazza Maggiore: **Furla** and
Gianfranco Ferre, via d'Azeglio; **Prada** and **Salvatore
Feragamo**, via Farini; **MaxMara** and **Stefanel**, via Rizzoli;
Giorgio, 29 via Santo Stefano.

The gleaming **Galleria Cavour** shopping mall off via Farini often
seems like a catwalk: **Gucci**, no.1, **T** 051-262981; **Versace**, no.2,
T 051-221016; **Emporio Armani**, no.9, **T** 051-238192.

Along **via dell'Indipendenza** are many funky shops with more
grungy and experimental fashions.

Paris Texas Italy, via Altabella 11, **T** 051-225741. *Map 4, C4 p256*
Dolce & Gabbana and Versace clothing and accessories at *dolce*
(sweet) prices.

Soho, via Volturno 7, **T** 051-270568. *Map 2, H7, p253* Cool presents.

Speedshop, via Zanardi 298, **T** 051-6347194. Label-less designer wear stockhouse.

Bruno Magli, via Large 23, **T** 051-6015011. Shoes for him and her and a few bags.

There are also a selection of stylish clothes shops between the bars and stalls of via Clavature, including **Diesel** in a former aristocratic palazzo, and under the arches of via Rizzoli for Bologna's branch of **Stefanel**. Prices are typically cheaper than in UK.

Clothing warehouses

A.N.G.E.L.O, Vintage Palace, via Garibaldi 59, Lugo di Ravenna, Ravenna, **T** 0545-35200. *Map 3, D7, p256* The Italian second-hand clothes mecca where you can pick up Chanel, Dior, Gucci, Pucci, you-name-it for knockdown prices.

Food

Tamburini, via Caprarie 1, **T** 051-234726. *Map 4, D5, p256* A mecca of savoury delights: meats, cheeses and various preparations of vegetables to take away.

Paolo Atti e Figli, via Caprarie 7, **T** 051-220425. *Map 4, D5, p256* All the region's different types of heavenly-smelling bread.

La Baita, via Pescherie Vecchie 3, **T** 051-223940. *Map 4, D4, p256* A shrine to all manner of pungent cheeses.

Antonio Paglione, via Orefici 23, **T** 051-220657. *Map 4, D4, p256* Vegetables and exotic fruits, and magnificent truffles when in season.

★ **Delicatessen heaven**
Bologna's exceptional food shops are a recipe for an expanded waist.

La Bottega del Caffè, via Orefici 6, **T** 051-236720. *Map 4, D4, p256* An aromatic array of different coffee types, ground before your nostrils.

Salumeria Bruno e Franco, via Oberdan 16, **T** 051-233692. *Map 4, C5, p256* Mouth-watering and wallet-weeping regional specialities.

Le Sfogline, via Belvedere 7, **T** 051-220558. *Map 2, H5, p252* Considered some of the best freshly made pasta in Bologna, ready to go or beautifully wrapped.

L'Adriatica, via Drapperie 8, **T** 051-228695. *Map 4, D5, p256* Locally (Rimini) caught fresh fish.

Majani, via De'Carbonesi 5, **T** 051-234302. *Map 3, C6, p256* Life is a chocolate box.

Al Regno della Forma, via Oberdan 45, **T** 051-233609. *Map 4, B5, p256* The nearest thing to Parmesan without actually going there. Great tyres of the stuff piled tantalizingly high.

Shopping

Markets

Mercato delle Erbe, via Ugo Bassi 2. *Mon-Sat 0700-1300 and 1700-1900, closed Thu and Sat pm.* Map 4, B1, p256 Covered market of vegetables, fruit and fish next door.

Via San Giuseppe, *second weekend every month except Jul and Aug.* Map 2, F7, p256 Arts and crafts under the Two Towers. Negotiate fairly.

Piazza Aldrovandi, *daily except Tue pm.* Map 4, E8, p256 Food, fruit and vegetables.

Piazza VIII Agosto, *weekly, Fri and Sat only.* Map 2, F8, p252 Household and leather goods.

Giardini della Montagnola, *timing as above.* Map 2, E8, p253 The city's main flea market in the park. Bargain hard.

Piazza Santo Stefano, *Sat and Sun, every second week.* Map 3, F12, p255 Antiques worth bargaining for.

Piazza di Porta Galliera, *daily in winter.* Map 3, F9, p255 Covered second-hand and antique book market.

Celo Celo Mamanca Map 4, B6, p256 Antiques and various ageing jumble every Thursday via Valdonica (the market's name literally means "I've got this, I've got this, but I haven't got…").

Music/CDs and records

Magazzini Nannucci, via Oberdan 7, **T** 051-237337. Map 4, B5, p256 Specializing in jazz, blues, soundtrack and world music. CD and vinyl.

Casa del Disco, via dell'Indipendenza 39, **T** 051-234224. *Map 2, G7, p253* .

Virgin, via Farini 13, **T** 051-276011. *Map 3, C8, 255* Multi-floored megestore.

Ricordi Mediastores, via Ugo Bassi 1-2, **T** 051-229604. *Map 4, C3, p256* Local branch of Italy's equivalent of Virgin.

Rock Shop, via della Grada 6, **T** 051-521551. *Map 2, H1, 252*
A quirky and attentive shop with an unusual selection of music.

Supermarket

Coin, via de' Carbonesi 7, **T** 051-238624. *Map 3, C6, p254* Bologna's main central supermarket with the remains of the Roman amphitheatre inconveniently uncovered right in the middle.

Wine

Enoteca Italiana, via Marsala 2, **T** 051-235989. *Map 2, H7, p253*
The best selection of regional and Italian wines in town. Tasting freely indulged. Good selections are also available at **Enoteca vini d'Italia** (see also p184), via Emilia Levante 142, **T** 051-541509 and **Enoteca Gilberto**, via Drapperie 5, **T** 051-223925. Avoid buying your wine in a supermarket if you can.

...a is well-equipped with facilities for all the ...al urban sporting pursuits such as football, tennis and swimming. From a spectator point of view the city also has football and basketball teams that are well worth watching.

Set in the lee of the Apennines, Bologna is perhaps surprisingly also a great place for more unusual outdoor and adventurous pursuits such as cross-country cycling, kayaking, hiking, rafting and, in winter, skiing.

As elsewhere in Italy, *il calcio* (football) in Bologna is followed like a religion and during the season you are liable to see men walking in silence in the park on Sunday afternoons with a radio attached to one ear listening to the game. It has been a while (1964) since Bologna FC won anything and only recently, courtesy of national icon Roberto Baggio, has the team begun to feature again as a major force, finishing in the top three of Serie A, Italy's premier division in the 01-02 season.

Basketball

Palacanestro (basketball) is the only sport that gets a look-in after football and Bologna's team, Virtus, is one of the best in Europe. They play at **PalaMalaguti**, via Cervia 1, in Casalecchio di Reno, southwest of the city, **T** 051-758758. You can but ticket at the stadium just before the match or by calling EBC, **T** 051-555504.

Football

Playing in red and blue stripes, Bologna's home ground is the **Stadio R Dall'Ara**, via A Costa 174, to the west of the Centro Storico, built in 1927 and one of Italy's first modern sports stadiums. League games are on Sundays and the tickets can be obtained from the ticket office, **T** 051-6111125 or *Carisbo*, **T** 051-4211342, the local bank which currently sponsors the team. Tickets cost upwards of €15 depending on where you want to sit.

If you're inspired by watching them, Bologna's parks are usually full of young boys trying to bend it like Baggio.

Golf

There are two courses within reach of central Bologna. A round of golf will cost upwards of €40 per person.

Gold Club Bologna, via Sabattini 69 in Monte San Pietro, **T** 051-969100. *Closed Mon.*
Golf Club Molino del Pero, via Molino del Pero 323 in Monzuno, **T** 051-6770506. *Closed Mon.*

Gyms

Palestra Refran, via del Fico 4, **T** 051-264596.

Centro Sportivo, piazza Azzarita.

Hiking

There are numerous trails mapped out in the hills with red triangles but it is best to obtain maps and the latest information from the tourist office or the CAI (Club Alpino Italiano), **T** 051-234856. The GEA (Grande Escursione Appenninica) is a 400 km trail mapped out in 1983 that traces the mountain range from Liguria to le Marche of which you might want to walk a section. There are various mountain refuges at which either to stop and eat or stay over. Rifugio Citta di Sarzana, **T** 0522-431166 is on the GEA. The CAI has details of others.

National parks

Around Bologna are numerous beautiful parks notable for their interesting geology and varied flora and fauna including many birds of prey. They also contain biking trails and have bike hire facilities. Contact the tourist office for more information about the following parks:

Il Parco dello Stirone, ambitiously likened to America's canyon country. **Parco dei Sassi di Rocca Malatina**, known for sandstone needles and peregrine falcons. **Parco dell'Alto Apennino Modenese**, eagle country. **Il Parco del Delta del Po**, 60 hectares of marshland and lagoons perfect for birdwatching.

★ **Bikes versus tortellini**
Bologna's 2-wheeled means of transport are a good antidote to the city's copious diet.

Skiing

In places the Apennines reach heights of 2,000 m, guaranteeing good snowfall in winter. It was on the slopes near Bologna that Alberto Tomba learnt to ski. There are over twenty well-equipped resorts in all, of which the following are the best.

Corno alle Scale/Budiara/Val Carlina 30 km of runs up to 1,945 m altitude. Downhill and cross-country skiing. 80 km from Bologna, accessible by train to Porretta.
Sestola 20 km of runs, downhill and cross-country. 67 km from Modena, accessible by train to Porretta.
Fiumalbo/Monte Cimone 16 km of runs, downhill and cross-country. Take the train to Pistoia.

Swimming pools

Bologna has a number of public swimming baths.
Bologna FC stadium complex, via Costa 174. *Daily 0930-1900.*
Cavina, via Biancolelli 36, **T** 051-247237.
Record, via del Pilastro 8, **T** 051-503311.
Silhouette, via Albiroli 5, **T** 051-237842.
Sterlino, via Murri 113, **T** 051-6237034.

Tennis

Centro Sportivo Record, via Pilastro 8, **T** 051-503311. Indoor and outdoor courts for between €6-€15, depending on peak or off-peak hours.

Gay and lesbian

In tune with its long-standing tradition for emancipated thinking, Bologna is one of the cities in Italy most open in its attitude towards homosexuality and has become regarded almost as a gay centre internationally. Bologna is the seat of the national gay movement and is considered to have reached 'the European level' of tolerance and understanding. The local council was the first in Italy to permit gay couples to apply for communal housing and Bologna was the first place in Italy to have a special Condomeria (a shop – now closed – dispensing prophylactics and advice on safe sex for both gays and heterosexuals). It has not always been a smooth ride: Pope John Paul II once condemned Emilia-Romagna as the most degenerate province in Italy partly on account of its gay tolerance. Rather than there being a defined structure much of the buzz of the city and its nightlife is fuelled by the gay community. That said, there are a number of places around the city which are specifically viewed as gay meeting points. A good website is www.gaybologna.net

Associations

KGB, the amusing acronym for the Komitato Gay di Bologna (contactable through www.gaybologna.net) is an internet-based meeting place, chat forum and association which organizes parties, dinners, events and shows for the local gay community.

ARCI-Gay – an organization of some 15,000 members, famously more than the Republican Party according to its President, Franco Grillini.

Ufficio Progetto Donna, via Santa Margherita 13, **T** 051-271457. A newly founded organization catering specifically for the lesbian community and also feminist interest, organising meetings, events and discussions.

Bars and clubs

Gay Zen Café, via Mascarella 79, **T** 0338-2221993. *2200-0130*. A relaxed hangout for a quiet drink, frequented by both gay. and straight males and females

Cassero, piazza di Porta Lame. *2130-0200*. Sun night disco, Thu Les.Bo (lesbian) night. Also seat of the above ARCI-Gay gay and lesbian organization. This used to be under the Porta Saragozza where it attracted controversy since it is also through this gate that the holy San Luca icon passes once a year.

Planet Girl, via Stefani, San Giovanni in Persiceto (*outside Bologna*). Not exactly central but a cosy retreat in the form of a bar-cum-club for girls only.

Da Renzo e Andrea, via L/ Spada 28, **T** 0349-5587077. Da Renzo e Andrea – a favourite place for a snack and drink among gays.

Pachito, via Polese 47, **T** 051-243998. *2230-0400*. A small and dark nightclub frequented exclusively by gays.

Kinky, via Zamboni. *In winter only, closes in June for summer*.

Gay-friendly hotels

Il Guercino, via L Serra 7, **T** 051-369853 (p132). **Hotel Marconi**, via Marconi 22, **T** 051-262832 (p132).

Language

The accepted and neutral word for 'gay' in Italian is *froccio* or alternatively 'gay'.

Radio

The local radio station, **Radio Città del Capo**, on 96.25fm, has a gay hour from 2200-2330 every night.

Gay-friendly restaurants

Da Nino, via Volturno 9. **Amadeo**, via Saragozza 88, **T** 051-585060. **Speedy Pizza**, via Saragozza 25, **T** 051-585203.

Saunas

New Vigour Sauna, via San Felice 6, **T** 051-232507. *1430-0300*. **Cosmos**, via Boldrini 16. *1400-0130*.

Rivalled only by food and their own appearance, children are the number one priority among Italians. Far from presenting a problem, you are more likely to endear yourself to the locals if you have children with you than annoy them. Children are welcome everywhere. At *passeggiata* and *aperitivo* time they are paraded around on the shoulders of proud fathers. They are taken out to restaurants and allowed to stay up late with the adults. In 2000, to coincide with their tenancy of the European City of Culture mantle, the council launched a special initiative called 'The City for Kids' which opened up galleries and theatres to Bologna's children and created workshops and exhibition spaces for them to indulge their creativity. This has left an important legacy whereby significant concessions are still offered to children for entry into museums and galleries, differing according to age group. The development of the ex-Sala Borsa into a multimedia library (see p48) was specifically aimed at encouraging children to interact with local history and culture.

Bologna

While most of the fine art, churches and architecture may leave children cold, they might find some of the university museums more interesting, in particular **La Specola** (see p56), the nearest thing Bologna has to a planetarium, housing telescopes and other complicated old instruments for star-gazing. **Il Museo delle Navi** (see p57) has beauifully delicate models of 17th- and 18th-century warships. **Il Museo di Architettura Militare** (see p57) has intricately carved models of armaments and toy soldiers.

Basilica di San Petronio (see p34) While any child might be inspired by its sheer size, young curiosity is likely to be aroused by the astronomical clock.

La Torre degli Asinelli The climb up might be a bit steep but energetic children will enjoy the view from the top (p49).

★ **Long way down**
The views from the top of the Torre degli Asinelli, of the roofs of Bologna and the Italian peninsula from the Alps to the Adriatic, are well worth the long climb up.

Casa Isolani There are plenty of amusing things for children to find in Bologna such as the arrows stuck in the wooden arcade above this house (see p67).

Palazzo Re Enzo Let children discover and enjoy the acoustic effect at the crossroads under the belfry (see p40).

If little feet grow tired of traipsing around Bologna, a good way to show them the city while also giving them the exhilaration of a fair ride is by taking them up in the **static balloon** which climbs 150 m above the city from the Giardini Margherita (see Tours p30).

The **Giardini Margherita** and the **Giardini della Montagnola** are good places to take children for a picnic or to let them let off steam on the lawns and among the trees.

Bologna also has a number of swimming pools and tennis courts that might keep art-weary children happy (see Sports p205).

Outside Bologna

Italia in Miniatura, via Popilia 239, Viserba di Rimini, **T** 0541-732004, www.italiainminiatura.com *16km north of Rimini on the SS16. Viserba* is a theme park showing pint-size versions of all the famous sights of Italy from piazza San Marco in Venice to the leaning tower of Pisa. There are also go-karts, a monorail and a Pinocchio ride. Contact tourist information for more details.

Acquafan, via Pistoia, Riccione, **T** 0541-605709. *1000-1830, Jun-mid Sep.* Riccione south of Rimini, is a swimming complex of wave pools, children's pools, grassy areas and kids play areas. Then there are always the beaches at Rimini itself.

Directory

Airline offices

Many airlines have call centre numbers instead of offices in the city. **American Airlines**, via Marconi 32 **T** 051-6492113. **British Airways**, **T** 199-712266. **Air France**, **T** 848878510. **Alitalia**, via Riva di reno 65, **T** 848865641. **Delta Airlines**, **T** 800-864114. **Go T** 848887766. **Lufthansa**, **T** 051-6477711. **KLM**, **T** 02-58580245. **SAS**, **T** 055-2382701. **United Airlines**, **T** 02-861831.

Airport Information

Marconi International Airport T 051-6479615 (*0630-2330*), **F** 051-6479719, www.bologna-airport.it **Forlì T** 0543-474990, **F** 0543-474909, www.forli-airport.it

Banks and ATMs

Banks are open from 0830-1330 and 1430-1530 on weekdays. Closed Sat and Sun. Cash machines are available at most banks and accept Visa, Cirrus, Eurocheque and other international cards. The city's main bank branches are along the axes via dell'Indipendenza, via Rizzoli, via Ugo Bassi.

Bicycle hire

Abycar, piazza Medaglie d'Oro 3 **T** 051-253 832 or **Senzauto**, also at the train station, **T** 051-251 401. Prices start at €5.20 per day for a bicycle (bicicletta) and €32 per day for a scooter (motorino). A deposit of €150 or €515 euros respectively is payable on hire.

Car hire

The following companies all have offices at the airport and also downtown, all along the northern end of via Marconi/via Amendola.
Avis, viale Pietramellara 35, **T** 051-255024. **Europcar**, via Masini 4, **T** 051-254126. **Hertz**, via Amendola 17-22, **T** 051-254830. **Maggiore**, **T** 051-252525. **Sixt**, **T** 051-255546.

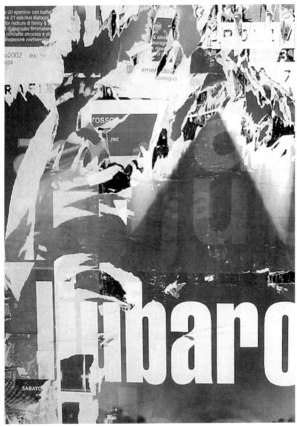

★ Strada dell'arte

Around the university on via Zamboni and via delle Belle Arti, the walls are bespattered with posters and graffiti announcing artistic, musical and theatrical events.

Consulates

Bologna has consulates for a number of countries. **Austria**, via Ugo Bassi 13, **T** 051-268711. **Belgium**, viale Repubblica 13, **T** 051-505101. **France**, via Guerazzi 1, **T** 051-230505. **Germany**, piazza Calderini 2, **T** 051-273790. **Holland**, via Clavature 22, **T** 051-234115. **South Africa**, via Saragozza 12, **T** 051-331306.

Credit Card Lines

Amex T 06-72900347. **Diners T** 800-8864064. **Mastercard T** 800-870866. **Visa T** 800-877232.

Cultural Institutions

Bologna has branches of many Italian institutes linked to different countries.

Italy-Holland, via Castiglione 34, **T** 051-234246. **Italy-France**, via de Marchi 4, **T** 051-332828. **Italy-America**, via Belmeloro 11, **T** 051-262825. **Italy-Ireland**, via San Vitale 96, **T** 051-224372. **British Council**, strada Maggiore 27, **T** 051-221249. **Italy-Germany**, strada Maggiore 29, **T** 051-225658. **Italy-Israel**, via Polese 28, **T** 051-246063.

Dentists

Contact the main hospital (see below)

Disabled

Italy is a bit behind when it comes to catering for the disabled but Bologna is better than most Italian cities. Contact an agency before departure for more details such as Accessible Italy, www.accessibleitaly.com, or Vacanze Serene **T** 800271027.

Doctors

Contact main hospital (see below). EU citizens should take their E111 with them.

Electricity
Italy functions on a 220V mains supply.

Embassies
See under Consulates.

Emergency Numbers
Police **T** 112. Ambulance **T** 113, **T** 118 or **T** 333333. Fire **T** 115. Red Cross **T** 118.

Hospitals
The city's main hospital is Santa Orsola on via Massarenti 8, to the east of the city, **T** 051-6363 111. Other hospitals: Bellaria **T** 051-6225111; Maggiore **T** 051-6478111; Malpighi **T** 051-6362111; Rizzoli **T** 051-63 66111.

Internet
Sala Borsa, piazza Nettuno 3, **T** 051-204400. *Tue-Sat 0900-1900, Mon 1430-1900*. **Sportello Iperbole**, piazza Maggiore 6, **T** 051-203184. *Mon-Sat 0930-1830*. **Informagiovani**, via P. de Crescenzi 14, **T** 051-525842. *Daily 1000-1300, 1500-1800*. **Link Project**, via Fioravanti 14, **T** 051-370971. *Wed-Sat, 2200 onwards*. **Inter Media**, via Ranzani 5/12, **T** 051-247247. *Daily, all day*.

Left luggage
The left hand bulding of the railway station on piazza Medaglie d'Oro has both manned and locker left luggage services.

Libraries
The city's main public library is the **Biblioteca dell'Archiginnasio**, piazza Galvani 1, **T** 051-276811, open Mon-Fri 0900-1900, Sat 0900-1400. **Ex-Sala Borsa**, piazza Maggiore – Bologna's new multimedia library. *Currently closed for refurbishment*. **Biblioteca Universitaria**, via Zamboni 33,

T 051-2099360. *Mon-Fri 0830-1730, Sat and Sun 0900-1830. Main university library.*

Lost property
Lost property can be claimed at the lost property office in via dell'Industria 2, **T** 051-6018623, or at the railway station lost property office **T** 051-6302354.

Motorcycle hire (see bicycle hire)

Media
English and other language newspapers are available from kiosks at the station and around the main squares of piazza Maggiore and piazza Minghetti.

Italian television has seven terrestrial channels with occasional good programmes between the topless chat shows.

The local newspaper is called the *Resto del Carlino* (named after the value of the change you used to get from buying a Carlino cigar).

Pharmacies (late night)
There is a large late-night pharmacy to the west of the station and also the Farmacia Comunale at piazza Maggiore 6, **T** 051-239690. If it is not open, a list on the door has details of the rotation of open pharmacies. For an emergency pharmacist call the Farmaco Pronto on **T** 800-218489.

Police
The HQ of the Bologna carabinieri is at piazza Galileo 7, **T** 051-278846. Police emergency telephone is **T** 112.

Post offices
The city's main poste restante occupies the northern side of piazza Minghetti, open Mon-Fri 0815-1830, Sat 0815-1300. The hours of

business for smaller offices are 0830-1330, Mon-Sat. A first class stamp costs €0.62, €0.41 for a postcard. Postcards arrive quicker if you put them in an envelope. Call **T** 160 for information on other rates.

Public holidays
1st Jan, New Year's Day; 6th Jan, Epiphany; 25th April, Liberation Day; 1st May, Labour Day; 15th August, Assumption; 1st Nov, All Saints; 8th December, Immaculate Conception; 25th Dec, Christmas; 26th Dec, St Stephen's.

Religious services
San Pietro cathedral, via dell'Indipendenza 7, **T** 051-222112. *0730, 0930, 1030, 1130, 1230, 1730.* **San Petronio**, piazza Maggiore. *0815, 0900, 1000, 1100, 1200 and 1800.* **Santo Stefano**, via Santo Stefano 24, **T** 051-223256. *0830, 1030, 1130 and 1230.* **San Domenico**, piazza San Domenico 13, **T** 051-6400411. *0900, 1030, 1200, 1800 and 2200.* **San Francesco**, piazza San Francesco, **T** 051-221762. *0730, 0900, 1100, 1200 and 1800.* **Santa Maria dei Servi**, piazzetta dei Servia, **T** 051-226807. *0930, 1100, 1200, 1900 and 2115.* **Santa Maria della Vita**, via Clavature 10, **T** 051-236245. *1900.* **San Giacomo Maggiore**, piazza Rossini **T** 051-225970. *0700, 0900, 1100, 1200 and 1700.* **San Luca**, via di San Luca, **T** 051-6142339. *0700, 0800, 0900, 1000, 1100 1200 and 1630.*

Student organizations
ARCI – membership can be made at any one of the clubs and bars belonging to this association, allowing entry to all other ARCI-affiliated locations. ARCI-GAY – contact Cassero at Porta Lame (see p213).

Telephone
The city's dialing code is 051 and must be dialed before all

numbers, even within the city. The prefix for Italy is +39. You no longer need to drop the initial '0' from area codes when calling from abroad. For directory enquiries call **T** 12.

Tipping
Only the more expensive restaurants will necessarily expect a tip though everywhere will be grateful for one. Ten to fifteen per cent is the norm. A few spare coins when ordering a coffee might speed the process up. Taxis may add on extra costs for you anyway but a little extra is always appreciated. Rounding prices up always goes down well, especially if it means avoiding having to give change, not a favourite Italian habit.

Toilets
There are public toilets at the railway station and also just off the southwest corner of piazza Maggiore on via IV Novembre. Otherwise you can use the toilets in bars and cafés although it is polite to ask (you may need to get a specific key) and sometimes necessary buy a drink or sandwich first.

Transport enquiries
Airport enquiries **T** 051-311578. Bus enquiries **T** 051-248374. Train enquiries **T** 051-246490, www.trenitalia.com.

Travel agents
Bigtours, via de Monari 2, **T** 051-239950/238411. *Viaggi Salvadori 1929*, via Ugo Bassi 13, **T** 051-225686/226493. *Hotelplan Italia*, via Santo Stefano, **T** 051-263601. *Citalia*, Marco Polo House 3-5 Lansdowne Rd, Croydon, UK, **T** +44-208-686 5533. *Fine Art Travel*, 15 Savile Row, London, UK, **T** +44-207-4378553. *Arlbaster & Clarke Wine Tours*, UK, www.arlbasterandclarke.com **T** +44-1730-893344.

A sprint through history

c1000 BC   First signs of human settlement around Bologna and the Apennines by the Villanova civilization.

c650-450 BC   Etruscans found Felsina on site of modern-day Bologna, then capital of northern Etruria.

450-191 BC   Felsina falls to the Gauls.

187 BC   Construction of the via Emilia begins.

189 BC   Romans defeat the Gauls and found the colony of Bononia. It suffers a great fire under Claudius but is rebuilt and enlarged under Nero.

431-450 AD   In the vacuum left by the decline of the Roman Empire, Bishop Petronius maintains the city under his bishopric and establishes the city's early boundaries.

476   The Western Roman Empire falls.

493-526   Bologna falls into the hands of the Goths under Theodoric.

554   The Byzantines take over under Justinian, ruling from Ravenna.

680   Lombard rule begins under King Liutprand.

774   The Lombards battle with the Franks. Bononia falls to the Franks.

1076-1122   The Wars of the Investitures mark the beginnings of a civic consciousness and the birth of communal power. The Guastalla Council, formed in 1106 frees Bologna from the jurisdiction of the archbishops of Ravenna. When Countess Matilda Canossa, the last representative of Imperial authority dies,

	self-appointed consuls take over and the *Comune* is born.
1088	Founding of Bologna's university.
1123	The first Bolognese consulate is formed.
1176	Bologna agrees to be a subject of the Lombard League.
c. 1200	Bologna is established as an independent *Comune*.
1220-1250	Reign of Emperor Frederick II. Conflict between Guelfs (supporters of the Pope) and Ghibellines (supporters of the Emperor) captivates and divides Italy.
1249	The Battle of Fossalta. Frederick II's son, Re Enzo is captured and imprisoned in Bologna.
1278	Bologna surrenders to Papal rule.
1325	Fierce rivalry between Ghibelline Modena and Guelf Bologna reaches a head when the Modenesi steal a symbolic bucket, *la secchia rapita*, immortalized in a poem by Tasso.
1348	The Black Death kills almost half the population of Bologna, then numbering around 40,000 citizens.
1390	Construction of the Basilica di San Petronio begins.
1400-1445	Bologna is governed by warring family dynasties, notably the Bentivoglios.
1506	Through a plot between Pope Julian II and King Louis II of France the Bentivoglio lordship is overpowered and Papal troops capture Bologna. The city falls under papal control of Pope Julian II and the Bentivoglio palace is razed.

1572-85	Rule of Bolognese by Pope Gregory XIII in conjunction with a senate comprising 40 members of Bologna's noble families with hereditary senatorship. Bologna enjoys a period of great economic prosperity through its silk and hemp industries.
1630	An epidemic devastates Bologna, reducing its population from 72,000 to 59,000.
1796	Seven years after the French Revolution, Napoleon invades Bologna and frees the city from Papal rule, suppresses the churches and monasteries and establishes French rule.
1797	Bologna is absorbed into Napoleon's Cisalpine Republic and becomes its capital.
1815	Battle of Waterloo takes place and Napoleon is defeated and dethroned, unsettling the status quo.
1848	Revolution and new power struggles rage across Europe. The First War of Italian Independence leads to defeat by the Hapsburg Austrians.
1859	The Second War of Independence under General Garibaldi is more successful.
1861	The *Risorgimento* and proclamation of the unified Kingdom of Italy under King Vittorio Emanuele of Savoy. Turin is capital of the new Italy.
1922	Start of the Fascist regime under Mussolini.
1941	Italy enters the Second World War as an ally of Germany. Mass deportation of Bolognese Jews.
1943	Mussolini is deposed by a coup and hung out for all to see in Milan. Italy signs an armistice. Nazis occupy northern and central Italy.

Aug 1944	Fleeing Nazis massacre 1800 resistance partisans at Marzabotto.
Apr1945	The Allies liberate Bologna.
1946	The Italian Monarchy is abolished and the first Italian Republic declared. Centre-right Christian Democrats dominate Italian government for next 47 years. Bologna is the seat of the Italian Communist party.
1970	Bologna university is occupied by students in protest at government education reforms. The late 1970s and early 1980s re nicknamed the *anni di piombo* (years of lead) as extremists from the right and left reciprocate terrorist attacks.
1977	Bolognese students take to the streets in their local version of the 1968 Paris riots, protesting against creeping neo-fascism within the government and against neo-fascist splinter groups.
1980	Bologna station is bombed by right-wing terrorists. 84 civilians die.
1996	Bolognese University professor, Romano Prodi, leader of centre-left coalition L'Ulivio ('the olive tree') is appointed Prime Minister.
1999	Romano Prodi is elected Head of European Parliament.
Mar 2002	Marco Biagi, a Government Employment advisor is shot dead outside his home in Bologna. It is the first political violence in Italy for two decades.

Art and architecture

5th century BC	The most intact vestiges of Etruscan civilization in the area can be seen in the preserved settlement of Misa outside Marzabotto. Etruscan artefacts including bowls, tools and arms and architectural fragments recovered from the area around Bologna can be seen in the Museo Civico Archaeologico.
218 BC	Romans begin construction of the via Emilia between Placentia (Piacenza) and Arinium (Rimini) passing through what will be Bologna where via Ugo Bassi and via Rizzoli meet today. From Roman times until the present day motorway which largely follows its course, this road will make Bologna an important trade junction, central to its affluence and artistic and architectural richness.
189 AD	Founding of Roman settlement of Bononia (Bologna). The piazza Maggiore is the forum and central market place. This square and the grid of streets forming the Quadrilatero make up the entire extent of the original settlement. Only the narrow streets of the Quadrilatero remain of the Roman presence, together with a piece of the Roman amphiteatre found and still displayed on the site of the Coin department store on via d'Azeglio.
402	Ravenna is made capital of the declining western Empire and enjoys an Indian summer of power and culture manifested in Byzantine mosaic art.
5th century	Saint Petronius confirms Bologna's boundaries and commissions a number of buildings, most notably the seven churches of Santo Stefano, inspired by a visit to Jerusalem.

727	Lombards capture Bologna and set about a number of urban embellishments, notably extensions and adjustments to the church complex of Santo Stefano.
1088	Bologna university is founded and with it the rebirth of the city's modern-day identity. The city expands in a typically concentric medieval way fed by with cobbled radial streets such as via Castiglione and via Santo Stefano.
1099	Modena cathedral is begun marking a high point in Romanesque architecture.
1119	Among other towers, the present twin towers of Bologna are built. Around the same time the city takes on many of its medieval aspects, in particular the porticoes which are built in order to expand the city's capacity for the influx of foreign students. The second ring of the city wall, the Torresotto, is formed.
1221	The death of Saint Dominic in Bologna leads to the construction of the church of San Domenico, the founder of the Dominican Order a masterpiece of Roman-Gothic architecture and home to the famous and florid Gothic Arca over the saint's tomb, by Nicolo dell'Arca.
14th century	Taddeo Pepoli serves as diplomat between the Papal forces and civic urges of Bologna and effectively holds power. He commissions the construction of many grand palaces along via Castiglione such as the austere palazzo Pepoli.
1390	The first stone of the Basilica of San Petronio is laid.

15th century	The patronage of the ruling Bentivoglio family bestows many embellishments on the city, most notably the church of San Giacomo Maggiore. After their overthrow art and architecture enjoys the patronage of papal envoys from Rome who support the arts and in particular the university. The Archiginnasio university building is commissioned, partly to stop the completion of the designs for the Basilica di San Petronio
16th-17th centuries	Foundation of the Bolognese school of fine art by the Carracci family of painters in rejection of Mannerism, who, together with pupils and followers such as Guido Reni, are commissioned to decorate many of the noble houses and churches of the city. Bologna becomes an alternative centre to Florence for art and a rich source of commissions. The city also enjoys great civic affluence giving rise to many Baroque embellishments and gestures, best manifested in the extravagant building of the covered portico to San Luca. The third ring of city walls is built and the city takes on the aspect it largely maintains to this day.
18th century	Napoleon enters Italy and closes many monasteries, divesting them of many of their works of art. Many monasteries are turned into storehouses. The canvasses, sculptures and frescoes are collected together in one place to form the present-day Pinacoteca. Simultaneously the Accademia delle Belle Arti is founded in Bologna and the main seat of the university is moved to its current location to unify its

	proliferating faculties in one area of the city as an example of a campus.
19th century	The Parisian fashion for boulevards leads to the destruction of many towers and medieval buildings for the creation of 'modern' avenues such as via dell'Indipendenza, via Ugo Bassi, via Rizzoli and piazza di Porta Ravegnana. Bologna's canals and waterways are covered over and filled in.
20th century	Birth of Giorgio Morandi in Bologna. The artist, who would spend all of his life in and around the city eschews grandiose avant-garde modernism and abstract art for a parochial and delicate attempt to praise and triumph the simple and everyday things in nature.
1974	Federico Fellini makes *Amarcord*, a film based on and set in his birthplace, Rimini.
1980s	The exhibition centre is built. Designed by Kenzo Tange, its towers, which in any other city would be ordinary skyscrapers, are meant to reflect medieval Bologna's architectural leitmotif.
2000	Bologna is elected one of seven European cities of culture to mark the Millennium. A progressive local government ensures that Bologna's treasures are kept in a good state of repair and open to the public. The council supports many student art initiatives. A wing of the Palazzo Comunale is converted in a multi-media library aimed at bringing children closer to culture. Work begins on restoring the old port district into a cultural centre.

Books

Bologna does not generally feature as largely as Florence, Venice or Rome in the rose-tinted travels of 19th-century writers, dandies and Victorians on the Grand Tour. Mostly the city receives a cursory mention focused principally on the city's art treasures but the following are all good reads. Bologna also features in passing in the portraits of Italy by Jan Morris, D H Lawrence and Edith Wharton. Many of the older texts are available as free downloads from Project Gutenberg at http://promo.net/pg/

Travel writing

Byron, *Letters* (various volumes, 1798-1822) , Typically floral musings, extravagant statements and clever-dick comments in epistles to fellow novelists.

Dickens, C, *Pictures from Italy* (Penguin, 1866), Travelogue of incisive and refreshingly unblinkered observations and descriptions.

Goethe, W, *Italian Journey* (Penguin, 1786-1788) Beautifully written descriptions mixed with more abstract musings from the original Romantic smitten by Italy.

Morton, H V, *A Traveller in Italy* (Methuen, 1969) A gentlemanly and scholarly account infused with local detail and encounters with the natives.

Non-fiction

Barzini, L, *The Italians* (Penguin 1968) At times almost a character/nation assassination, all the more incredible in that it is written by an Italian. Possibly the most incisive piece of writing there is on the Italian mindset and the illusion that is Italy.

Best

★ **Bolognese food books:**

- *The Classic Italian Cookbook*, Marcella Hazan (Macmillan 1988) Exactly what is says on the tin – an indispensable starting point for Italian cuisine
- *The Gastronomy of Italy*, Anna del Conte (Pavilion 2001) A bible to the cuisine of all regions containing over 300 recipes
- *Lorenza's Italian Seasons*, Lorenza de' Medici (Pavilion 2001) A beautifully photographed tome on the use of seasonal produce according to the calendar of Italian feast-days
- *The Culture of Food* (Comune di Bologna, 2000) Recipes, restaurants from the Emilia-Romagna area
- *Emilia-Romagna* (Gambero Rosso) Yearly Italian guide with recipes and restaurants from the Italian equivalent of Michelin.

Richards , C, *The New Italians* (Penguin 1995), A refreshing account of Italy and the Italians at the end of the 20th century that dispels the myths of Chiantishire and Bella Tuscany.

Fiction
Leopardi , G, *Il Giardino dei Finzi-Contini*, Romantic novel set and written in and around Bologna, not available in translation.

Newby, E, *Love and War in the Apennines* (Picador 1983) Exactly what is says on the tin, but written with the wit and poignancy of the great travel writer.

Stendhal, H *Charterhouse of Parma* (Various publishers, 1839) Love, intrigue, jealousy and vanity set in the city of Parma.

Giosue Carducci The poetic works of the 1906 Nobel Prize winner are inspired, among other things, by his life in and around Bologna.

Language

Local dialect

99% of Bolognese can and generally do speak 'normal' Italian but don't be surprised if in the markets or some of the more down-at-heel osterias you can't understand what's being said. Italy's regional divisions are as marked in its language as in its cuisine, and each region has not only very distinct accents but also, due to Italy's comparative youth as a unified nation, living dialects which are far from extinction. The Bolognese accent is distinguishable for its nasal quality and for a tendency to pronounce the letter 's' as 'sh – think Sean Connery with an Italian accent. One local phrases you might hear in dropped into conversations are 'Bon allez', a vestige of Napoleonic occupation meaning 'basta' – 'enough!' and 'namo (short for 'andiamo') – 'let's go'.

Gestures

Italians are famously theatrical and animated in dialogue and often resort to a variety of gestures in order to accompany or in some cases substitute words. Knowing a few of these will help you both to understand what's being implied to you and also to become more Italian during your stay.

Side of left palm on side of right wrist as right wrist is flicked up   Go away

Hunched shoulders and arms lifted with palms of hands outwards   What am I supposed to do?

Thumb, index and middle finger of hand together, wrist upturned and shaking   What the hell are you doing/what's going on?

Both palms together and moved up and down in front of stomach   Ditto

All fingers of hand squeezed together   To signify a place is packed full of people

Front of side of hand to chin   To signify 'nothing', as in 'I don't

understand' or 'I've had enough'
Flicking back of right ear To signify someone is gay
Index finger in cheek To signify good food

Basics:
thank you *grazie*
hi/goodbye *ciao*
good day (until after lunch/mid-afternoon) *buongiorno*
good evening (after lunch) *buonasera*
goodnight *buonanotte*
goodbye *arrivederci*
please *per favore*
I'm sorry *mi dispiace*
excuse me *permesso*
yes *si*
no *no*

Numbers
one *uno*, two *due*, three *tre*, four *quattro*, five *cinque*, six *sei*, seven *sette*, eight *otto*, nine *nove*, 10 *dieci*, 11 *undici*, 12 *dodici*, 13 *tredici*, 14 *quattordici*, 15 *quindici*, 16 *sedici*, 17 *diciassette*, 18 *diciotto*, 19 *diciannove*, 20 *venti*, 21 *ventuno*, 22 *ventidue*, 30 *trenta*, 40 *quaranta*, 50 *cinquanta*, 60 *sessanta*, 70 *settanta*, 80 *ottanta*, 90 *novanta*, 100 *cento*, 200 *due cento*, 1000 *mille*.

Questions
how? *come?*
how much? *quanto?*
when? *quando?*
where? *dove?*
why? *perchè?*
what? *Che cosa?*

Problems

I don't understand *Non capisco*

I don't know *Non lo so*

I don't speak Italian *Non parlo italiano*

How do you say ...(in Italian)? *Come si dice ... (in italiano)?*

Is there anyone who speaks English? *C'è qualcuno che parla inglese?*

Shopping

this one/that one *questo/quello*

less *meno*

more *di più*

How much is it/are they? *quanto costa/costano?*

Can I have ...? *posso avere ...?*

Eating/drinking

Can I have the bill? *posso avere il conto?*

What's this? *cos'è questo?*

Is there a menu? *c'è un menù?*

Where's the toilet? *dov'è il bagno?*

Travelling

one ticket for... *un biglietto per...*

single *solo andata*

return *andata e ritorno*

does this go to Bologna? *questo va a Bologna?*

airport *aeroporto*

bus stop *fermata*

train *treno*

car *macchina*

taxi *tassi*

Hotels

a double/single room *una camera doppia/singola*
a double bed *un letto matrimoniale*
bathroom *bagno*
Is there a view? *c'è una bella vista?*
Can I see the room? *posso vedere la camera?*
When is breakfast? *a che ora è la colazione?*
Can I have the key? *posso avere la chiave?*

Conversation

alright *va bene*
right then *allora*
who knows! *bo! / chi sa?*
good luck! *in bocca al lupo!* (literally, 'in the mouth of the wolf')
one moment *un'attimo*
hello (when answering a phone) *pronto* (literally, 'ready')
let's go! *andiamo!*
enough/stop *basta!*
give up! *dai!*
I like ... *mi piace ...*
how's it going? (well, thanks) *come va?* (bene, grazie)
how are you? *come sta/stai?* (polite/informal)

Time

morning *mattina*
afternoon *pommeriggio*
evening *sera*
night *notte*
soon *presto/fra poco*
later *più tardi*
What time is it? *Che ore sono?*
today/tomorrow/yesterday *oggi/domani/ieri*

Index

A

Aalto, Alvar 107
Abbazia di Santa Maria 106
Accademia della Scienza 56
accommodation 119-134
Acquafan 218
Addobbi 195
Aipo 91
air travel 23
airline offices 220
airport information 220
airport, Forlì 24, 220
airport, Marconi International 24
alternative shopping 199
Amarcord 189
antiques 199
Antonioni, Michangelo 115
arcades 57
architecture 232
ARCI 225
art 232
Arte Fiera 91
astronomical clock 36
Autodromo Dino Ferrari 116
Automobile Club Italiano 25

B

Baccanale (Imola) 196
balloon rides 30
banks and ATMs 220

bars 169-186
Basilica dei Santi Vitale e Agricola 70
Basilica di San Petronio 217
Basilica di San Vitale 117
Basilica di Sant'Apollinaire Nuovo 117
basketball 207
Battistero 117
Bazzano 106
beaches 118
Bentivoglio family 78
Bernini 85
Biagi, Marco 70, 231
Bibbio Borso 111
Bibiena, Antonio 55
Bibiena, Francesco 85
Biblioteca Estense 111
Biblioteca Multimediale Sala Borsa 48
bicycle hire 220
Boccaccio 17
Bologna Sogna 196
Bolognina 91
books 236
bookshops 199
Borgo Panigale 92
Brigate Rosse 70
bus tours 29
bus travel 25, 27

C

Camera di San Paolo 108
Canaletto 109
canals 63
car hire 220

car travel 28
Carducci, Giosue 75, 98
Carnevale 195
Carracci family 234
Carracci, Agostino 85
Carracci, Annibale 53, 85 - 86
Carracci, Antonio 87
Carracci, Ludovico 38, 52, 54, 73, 82 - 83, 86
Casa Carducci 75
Casa Isolani 218
Casa Toscanini 109
Casa-torre Guidozagni 53
Case Isolani 67
Castel San Pietro 107
Castello di Serravalle 106
Castello Estense 113
Catedrale (Bologna) 45
CDs and records 204
cemetery 98
Cersaie 91
cheap eats 156
Chiesa dei Santi Gregorio e Siro 86
Chiesa del Corpus Domini 82
Chiesa del Sacro Cuore 92
Chiesa del San Sepolcro 71
Chiesa del Santissimo Crocefisso 70
Chiesa della Madonna del Baraccano 73
Chiesa della Madonna del Colombano 87
Chiesa della Madonna di

Galliera 85
Chiesa della Trinita 71
Chiesa di San Bartolomeo 52
Chiesa di San Domenico 73
Chiesa di San Francesco 81
Chiesa di San Giacomo Maggiore 53
Chiesa di San Giobbe 52
Chiesa di San Giovanni Evangelista 108
Chiesa di San Giovanni in Monte 72
Chiesa di San Martino 61
Chiesa di San Paolo in Monte 98
Chiesa di San Paolo Maggiore 83
Chiesa di San Procolo 79
Chiesa di Santa Lucia 76
Chiesa di Santa Maria dei Servi 71
Chiesa di Santa Maria l'Assunta 107
Chiesa di Santi Vitale e Agricola 65
Chiesa di Santo Stefano 69
Chiesa e Convento di San Salvatore 47
children 215
Cimabue 71
cinemas 189
clothes shopping 200
clubs 169-186
coffee 38
Colle dell'Osservanza 98

Collegio di Spagna 80
Collezioni Comunali d'Arte 38
comedy 189
Conservatorio della Madonna del Baraccano 73
Conservatorio di Musica G B Martini 55
Convento di Santa Lucia 76
Correggio 108
Corte Isolani 67
Cosmoprof 91
Costa, Lorenzo 54
credit card lines 222
Creti, Donato 96
cultural institutions 222

D
Dalla, Lucio 16
Dante 17, 51
Dante 58
de Modena, Giovanni 36
della Francesca, Piero 118
della Quercia, Jacopo 35, 54, 114
dell'Arca, Niccolo 37, 43, 72-73, 112
dentists 222
dialect 238
disabled 222
doctors 222
drinking 135-166
Due Torri 49
Duomo (Ferrara) 113
Duomo (Modena) 110
Duomo (Parma) 108

E
eating 135-168
electricity 223
embassies 223
emergency numbers 223
Erbario 59
Este dynasty 113
events 193
excursions 10
Exhibition Centre 90
Exhibition Centre 90

F
Fellini, Federico 189
Ferrara
  eating and drinking 168
  sights 113-115
  sleeping 134-135
Ferrari 112
Festa di San Luca 195
Feste della Laurea 195
Festivale dell'Estate (Modena) 196
festivals 193
Fontana del Nettuno 33
food shopping 201
football 207
Futureshow 91

G
Galleria Acquaderni 52
Galleria d'Arte Moderna 90
Galleria Estense 111
Galleria Ferrari 112
galleries list 101
Galvani, Luigi 77
gay 211-214
gestures 238

Ghetto Ebraico 52
Ghibellines 51
Giambologna 34
Giardini della Montagnola 218
Giardini di Margherita 100
Giardini Margherita 218
Giardini Pubblici della Montagnola 64
Giotto 60, 118
golf 207
Guelphs 51
Guercino 96
gyms 208

H
hiking 208
history 228-231
hospitals 223
hotels 119-134

I
Imola
    eating and drinking 168
    sights 116
    sleeping 134
internet points 223
Intimare 91
Italia in Miniatura 218

K
kids 215

L
La Torre degli Asinelli 217
language 238
Laureti, Tommaso 34
Lazzarina 41

left luggage 223
Leonardo da Vinci 109
Leopardi, Giacomo 68
lesbian 211
libraries 223
Lineapelle 91
Lippi, Filippino 73
Loggia della Mercanzia 66
lost property 224
Luna Park 91

M
Maranello 112
markets 203
Marzabotto massacre 37
Matricole 195
Mausoleo di Galla Placidia 117
media 224
Mercato del Pesce 87
Mercato delle Erbe 87
Metropolitana di San Pietro 45
Michelangelo 37
Minghetti, Marco 77
Mirasoli 78
Modena
    eating and drinking 168
    sights 110-115
    sleeping 133
Monastero degli Olivetani 99
Montefiorino 105
Monteveglio 106
mopeds 27
Morandi, Giorgio 40, 74, 98, 235
mosaics 117
Motorshow 91

Musei di Palazzo Poggi 56
Museo Archaeologico Nazionale Pompeo Aria 105
Museo Arcivescovile 117
Museo Bibliografico Musicale 55
Museo Civico Archeologico 44
Museo Civico del Risorgimento 75
Museo Civico Medioevale e del Rinascimento 85
Museo Crespellani, 106
Museo d'Arte Industriale 74
Museo d'Arte Medievale e Moderne e Etnologie 111
Museo del Patrimonio Industriale 101
Museo del Soldatino 101
Museo delle Navi 57
Museo di Anatomia Comparata 101
Museo di Anatomia Umana 59
Museo di Antropologia 101
Museo di Architettura Militare 58
Museo di Astronomia 57
Museo di Fisica 102
Museo di Geologia e Paleontologia 58
Museo di Mineralogia e Petrografia Luigi Bombucci 102
Museo di Zoologia 102

Museo Ebraico 102
Museo Morandi 39
Museo Ostretrico Giovanni Antonio Galli 58
Museo Storico dello Studio 102
Museo tattile di Pittura Antica e Moderna 102
museum passes 14
museums list 101
music 190

N

Napoleon 98, 108, 230, 234
Natale 196
national parks 208
newspapers 224
Nuovo Palazzo Bentivoglio 61

O

Oratorio di Santa Cecilia 54
Orto Botanico 59

P

Palazzina della Viola 59
Palazzo Albergati 82
Palazzo Bevilacqua 82
Palazzo Bolognini 67
Palazzo Caprara 47
Palazzo Comunale 36
Palazzo degli Affari e del Commercio 90
Palazzo dei Banchi 41
Palazzo dei Diamanti 115
Palazzo dei Musei 111
Palazzo dei Notai 41

Palazzo dell'Archiginnasio 43
Palazzo della Pilotta 109
Palazzo Ducale 109, 111
Palazzo Ercolani 75
Palazzo Fantuzzi 65
Palazzo Fava 84
Palazzo Finzi-Contini 68
Palazzo Grassi 62
Palazzo Magnani 53
Palazzo Malvezzi 53
Palazzo Marescalchi 48
Palazzo Marescotti 83
Palazzo Orsi 64
Palazzo Pepoli 76
Palazzo Pepoli Campogrande 76
Palazzo Podesta 39
Palazzo Re Enzo 39, 218
Palazzo Rusconi 83
Palazzo Salina 83
Palazzo Scagliarini-Rossi 65
Palazzo Schifanoia 114
Palio di San Giorgio 195
Palladio 77
Parco di Villa Ghigi 99
Parco Nord 91
Parma
  eating and drinking 168
  sights 108-109
  sleeping 134
parmesan 106
Parmigianino 108 - 109
Pavarotti, Luciano 16
Pepoli, Taddeo 60
Petrarch 17
pharmacies (late night) 224

piazza Galvani 43, 77
piazza Maggiore 33
piazza Malpighi 80
piazza Minghetti 77
Piazza Roosevelt 47
piazza San Domenico 72
piazza Santo Stefano 69
piazza VIII Agosto 63
Pinacoteca (Parma) 109
Pinacoteca Nazionale 60
Pinacoteca Nazionale (Ferrara) 115
Planetario 102
police 224
Porretta Terme 107
port district 88
Porta Galliera 88
Porta Saragozza 82
Portico di San Luca 93
Porto 89
post offices 224
Proculus 79
Prodi, Romano 231
public holidays 225

Q

Quadrilatero 42

R

rail travel 26
Ravenna 115
religious services 225
Reni, Guido 48, 52, 60, 72-73, 87, 96, 112, 234
Respighi, Ottorino 98
restaurants 135
Rimini
  bars and clubs 186
  eating and drinking 168

Rimini cont
   sights 118
   sleeping 134
road travel 25
Rocca di Vignola castle
   106
Rocca Sforzesca 116
Rocchetta Mattei 106
Rossi, Vasco 16

S

Saiedue 91
Saint Petronius 68
Sala Farnese 38
Salsomaggiore Terme 107
San Girolamo della
   Certosa 98
San Luca, Santuario della
   Madonna di 95
San Michele in Bosco 99
Sana 91
Santuario della Madonna
   di San Luca 95
Santuario di Santa Maria
   della Vita 43
sfogline 145
shopping 197-204
skiing 210
sleeping 119-134
spaghetti Bolognese 155
spas 107
specialities 149
Specola dell'Osservatorio
   Astronomico 57
sport 205
Stadio R Dall'Ara 190, 207
station (Bologna) 86
strada Maggiore 67, 74
student organisations 225

supermarket 204
swimming pools 210

T

Tange, Kenzo 235
taxis 29
Teatro Anatomico 44
Teatro Arena del Sole 87
Teatro Comunale 55, 190
Teatro Corso 68
Teatro Farnese 109
Teatro Regio 109
Teatro Romano 83
Teatro Testoni 92
telephone 225
television 224
Tempio Malatestiano 118
ten of the best 11
tennis 210
theatre 192
Tibaldi 77
Tiepolo 109
Tintoretto 39
Tipping 226
Titian 60
toilets 226
Torre degli Asinelli 49
Torre degli Azzoguidi 53
Torre degli Uguzzoni 52
Torre Garisenda 49
Torre Ghirlandia 111
Torre Prendiparte 52
Torresotto 65
Toscanini 109
tourist information 30
tours 29
Trade fairs 91
train travel 28
transport enquiries 226

travel agents 226
Two Towers 49

V

Vecchione 196
via Barberia 83
via Broccaindosso 65
via Castiglione 76
via del Porto 88
via del Pratello 81
via delle Moline 63
via Emilia 75
via Galliera 85
via San Vitale 64
via Santo Stefano 68
Vignola 106
Villa Aldini 98
Villa delle Rose 97
Villa Ghigi 99
Villa Spada 97
Viva Bologna 196

W

walking 208
walking tours 29
wine shopping 204
wine tours 30

Z

Zona Fiere 90
Zoo Acquario 116

Credits

Footprint credits

Text editor: Julius Honnor
Series editor: Rachel Fielding

Production: Jo Morgan, Mark Thomas
In-house cartography: Claire Benison,
Kevin Feeney, Robert Lunn,
Sarah Sorensen
Proof-reading: Sarah Thorowgood

Design: Mytton Williams
Maps: adapted from original cartography
by Netmaps SA, Barcelona, Spain

Photography credits

Front cover: Alamy
Inside: Julius Honnor
Generic images: John Matchett
Back cover: Julius Honnor

Print

Manufactured in Italy by LegoPrint
Pulp from sustainable forests

Publishing information

Footprint Bologna
1st edition
Text and maps © Footprint Handbooks
Ltd November 2002

ISBN 1 903471 50 8
CIP DATA: a catalogue record for this
book is available from the British Library

® Footprint Handbooks and the Footprint
mark are a registered trademark of
Footprint Handbooks Ltd

Published by Footprint Handbooks
6 Riverside Court
Lower Bristol Road
Bath, BA2 3DZ, UK
T +44 (0)1225 469141
F +44 (0)1225 469461
discover@footprintbooks.com
www.footprintbooks.com

Distributed in the USA by
Publishers Group West

Every effort has been made to ensure
that the facts in this pocket Handbook
are accurate. However the authors and
publishers cannot accept responsibility
for any loss, injury or inconvenience
sustained by any traveller as a result of
information or advice contained in this
guide.

Complete title list

Latin America & Caribbean

Argentina
Barbados (P)
Bolivia
Brazil
Caribbean Islands
Central America & Mexico
Chile
Colombia
Costa Rica
Cuba
Cusco & the Inca Trail
Dominican Republic
Ecuador & Galápagos
Guatemala
Havana (P)
Mexico
Nicaragua
Peru
Rio de Janeiro
South American
  Handbook
Venezuela

North America

Vancouver (P)
Western Canada

Africa

Cape Town (P)
East Africa
Libya
Marrakech &
  the High Atlas
Morocco
Namibia
South Africa
Tunisia
Uganda

Middle East

Egypt
Israel
Jordan
Syria & Lebanon

Asia

Bali
Bangkok & the Beaches
Cambodia
Goa
India
Indian Himalaya
Indonesia
Laos
Malaysia
Myanmar (Burma)
Nepal
Pakistan
Rajasthan & Gujarat
Singapore
South India
Sri Lanka
Sumatra
Thailand
Tibet
Vietnam

Australasia

Australia
New Zealand
Sydney (P)
West Coast Australia

Europe

Andalucía
Barcelona
Berlin (P)
Bilbao (P)
Bologna (P)
Copenhagen (P)
Croatia
Dublin (P)
Edinburgh (P)
England
Glasgow
Ireland
London
Madrid (P)
Naples (P)
Northern Spain
Paris (P)
Reykjavik (P)
Scotland
Scotland Highlands
  & Islands
Spain
Turkey

(P) denotes pocket
Handbook

For a different view…
choose a Footprint

Over 80 Footprint travel guides
Covering more than 145 of the world's most exciting
countries and cities in Latin America, the Caribbean, Africa, Indian
sub-continent, Australasia, North America, Southeast Asia, the
Middle East and Europe.

Discover so much more…
The finest writers. In-depth knowledge. Entertaining and accessible.
Critical restaurant and hotels reviews. Lively descriptions of all the
attractions. Get away from the crowds.

Maps

Quartiere Fieristico

Giardino Donatori del Sangue

Giardino G. Rossa

Via Corticella
Via di Saliceto
Via Corticella
Via Saliceto
Via Stalingrado
Viale Aldo Moro
Viale della Fiera

Via Bolognese Mazza
Via dall'Arca
Via Ferrarese

Piazza dell'Unità

Teatro Testoni

Chiesa del Sacro Cuore

Viale della Repubblica
Via Donato

Stazione Centrale F.S.
Piazza XX Settembre
Piazza di Porta Galliera

Via A. Silvani
Mura di Porta Lame
Piazza Sette Novembre 1944
Giardino del Cavaticcio

Giardini Publicci Della Montagnola

Palazzo Pepoli

Via Masini
Viale C. Bert Pichat

Orto Botanico
Palazina de la Viola
Museo di Anatomia Umana

Piazza di P.ta S. Donato
Stazione F.S. S. Vitale

Giardino Decorato Valor Civile

Largo Gaduti del Lavoro

Teatro Arena del Sole

Via dell'Independenza

Chiesa dell'Abadia

Chiesa del Santi Gregorio e Siro

Palazzo Grassi

Nuevo Palazzo Bentivoglio

Pinacoteca Nazionale

Teatro Comunale

Musei di Palazzo Poggi

Viale Q. Filopanti
Mura G. Zamboni

Chiesa di San Francesco

Via Ugo Bassi

Metropolitana di San Pietro

Palazzo Caprara
Palazzo Comunale

Torre degli Asinelli e Garisenda

Palazzo Malvezzi

Piazza di Porta S. Vitale

Via Massarenti

Via Pelagio Pelagi

Piazza Malpighi
Sant'Isaia

Piazza Maggiore

Via S. Vitale

San Michele

Piazza Aldrovandi

Palazzo Ercolani

San Petronio
La Casa Isolani

La Chiesa di Santo Stefano
Piazza Santo Stefano

Piazza di Porta Maggiore

Collegio di Spagna
Palazzo Bevilacqua
Palazzo Albergati

Palazzo dell'Archiginnasio
Piazza S. Domenico

S. Giovanni in Monte

Via Santo Stefano

Casa Carducci
Piazza Dante G. Carducci

Piazza Trento e Trieste

Chiesa di San Procolo

Chiesa di San Domenico

Il Palazzo di Giustizia

Piazza Morandi

Via Mazzini

P.za di P.ta S.Mamolo
Viale E. Panzacchi

Piazza Baraccano

Via G. Gozzadini

Via Lana
Via Augusto Murri
Via Mezzofa

Via S. Mamolo

Giardinni Scoto

Chiesa di S. Michele in Bosco

Piazza Porta Castiglione

Porta di Santo Stefano

Piazza di P.ta S.Stefano

Giardini Margherita

P. le Jaccia

251

Map 2

Canale Navile

Via de Carracci

Via Francesco Zanardi

Via Bovi Campeggi

Viale P. Pietramella

Casarini

Via Tanari

Via De La Bova

Via Cipriani

Via Pietro

Via Ranuzzi

Via Parmeggiani

Viale

Via E. Fl. Cairoli

Via Milazz

Via Amendola

Via C.

Via Scalo

Via Berti

Via L. De Crescenzi

Piazza VII Novembre 1944

Mura di Porta Lame

Via Don Rosselli

Via Minzoni

Piazza dei Martiri 1943-45

Via dello

Via Malvasia

Via Marcello

Giardino del Cavaticcio

Via del Porto

Ghisiliera

Silvani

Via Dolfi

Via Azzo

Via Gardino

Via Rondone

Largo Gaduti del Lavoro

Fontanina

Via Polese

Palazzo D. Regione

Viale A. Battistelli

De Liuzzi

Via Graziano

Via Calori

Ercolani

Cervellati

Via delle Lame

Via del Pagliac

Tanari Vecc

Ambrosini

Via Aurelio Saffi

Giardino Decorato Al Valor Civile

Mura P.ta S. Felice

Piazza Azzarita

Via Nannetti

Padre Brughol

Via Grimaldi

Via Marconi

Quinto

Piazza Porta S. Felice

Piazza Resistenza

Via Riva Reno

Via Riva Reno

S. Lorenzo

Grabinski

S. Maria Magg

Schiavonia

Viale G. Vicini

Via Monaldo

Via della Grada

Via San Felice

Protiche

Chiesa dell'Abadia

Casse Maggia Maiani

Via S. Giorgio

Via S. Croce

S. Valentino

S. Rocco

Via Pietralata

Via Paradiso

di Cabalini

Otto Colonne

Belvedere

Chiesa del Santi Gregorio e Siro

Via Parigi

Gessi

Via Ugo B

Via Monte

Usberti

Zambeccari

Pacchioni

Muratori

Calari

252

P.ta S. Isaia

Via del

Pratello

Via S. Francesco

Chiesa di San

Mercato delle Erbe **Pala**

Maps

253